School District of Hillsborough County
ACCELERATED MATHEMATICS

Metro Math
VOYAGES

Grade 5 → 6   ANCHORS

TOPICS 6 and 7

PROPERTY OF LIMONA ELEM.

Senior Authors: Jack Beers, Al Soriano

Design: Debrah Welling

Cover Photograph: The Tampa Bay Convention
& Visitors Bureau

D1313785

Metropolitan Teaching and Learning Company
33 Irving Place
New York, NY 10003

ISBN 1-58830-811-1

Table of Contents

TOPIC 6:
Fractions, Mixed Numbers, and Percent

Lesson (Benchmark)	Page Number
1 Multiples and Common Multiples (MA.A.5.2.1)	1
2 Factors and Common Factors (MA.A.5.2.1)	5
3 Divisibility (MA.A.5.2.1)	9
4 Prime and Composite Numbers (MA.A.5.2.1)	13
5 Patterns with Square Numbers (MA.A.5.2.1)	17
6 Set Comparisons (MA.A.1.2.3)	21
7 Parts of a Whole (MA.A.1.2.4)	25
8 Equivalent Fractions (MA.A.1.2.4)	29
9 Renaming Fractions and Mixed Numbers (MA.A.1.2.4)	33
10 Renaming Fractions, Decimals, and Percents (MA.A.1.2.4)	37
11 Approximating Fractions (MA.A.1.2.2)	41
12 Comparing Fractions, Decimals, and Percents (MA.A.1.2.2)	45
13 Adding and Subtracting Fractions (MA.A.3.2.3)	49
14 Adding and Subtracting with Fractions, Mixed Numbers, and Whole Numbers (MA.A.3.2.3)	53
15 Adding and Subtracting Mixed Numbers (MA.A.3.2.3)	57
16 Estimating Sums and Differences of Fractions and Mixed Numbers (MA.A.4.2.1)	61
17 Adding and Subtracting Unlike Fractions (MA.A.3.2.3)	65
18 Adding Unlike Fractions and Mixed Numbers (MA.A.3.2.3)	69
19 Subtracting Unlike Fractions and Mixed Numbers (MA.A.3.2.1)	73
20 Computing with Fractions, Decimals, and Percents (MA.A.3.2.3)	77
21 Finding a Fraction of a Number (MA.A.3.2.1)	81
22 Multiplying Whole Numbers and Fractions (MA.A.3.2.1)	85
23 Multiplying by a Fraction (MA.A.3.2.1)	89
24 Percent of a Number (MA.A.3.2.1)	93
25 Multiplying with Mixed Numbers (MA.A.3.2.1)	97

TOPIC 7:
Probability and Statistics

Lesson (Benchmark)	Page Number
1 Outcomes (MA.E.2.2.2)	1
2 Experiments (MA.E.2.2.1)	5
3 Probability (MA.E.2.2.2)	9
4 Making Inferences from Outcomes (MA.E.2.2.2)	13
5 Spinner Predictions (MA.E.2.2.2)	17
6 Using Graphs to Find Probability (MA.E.2.2.1)	21
7 Listing and Counting Possible Outcomes (MA.E.2.2.1)	25
8 More About Probability (MA.E.2.2.1)	29
9 The Range and the Mode of a Set (MA.E.1.2.2)	33
10 The Mean and the Median of a Set (MA.E.1.2.2)	37

TOPIC 6

Fractions, Mixed Numbers, and Percent

Multiples and Common Multiples

REACHING MY GOAL
Find the least common multiple of two or more whole numbers. (MA.A.5.2.1)

How did I do?

A. When you multiply a number by a whole number, the product is a **multiple** of the original number.

Example 1

Which of the numbers 78, 82, and 6 are multiples of 6?

Think: ? × 6 = 78

$$\begin{array}{r} 13 \\ 6\overline{)78} \end{array}$$

13 × 6 = 78
So, 78 is a multiple of 6.

Think: ? × 6 = 82

$$\begin{array}{r} 13 \text{ R}4 \\ 6\overline{)82} \end{array}$$

So, 82 is not a multiple of 6.

Think: ? × 6 = 6

1 × 6 = 6

So, 6 is a multiple of 6.

> **THINK**
> If there is a remainder, the dividend is not a multiple of the divisor.

B. Nonzero multiples of two or more numbers are **common multiples** of those numbers. The common multiple with the least value is the **least common multiple** or **LCM**.

Example 2

Which numbers less than 50 are common multiples of 6 and 8?
What is the LCM of 6 and 8?

Step 1: You can use either repeated addition or multiplication to find the multiples of 6 and 8. Use addition:

+6 +6

0…6…12…18… 24 … 30 … 36 … 42 … 48

+8 +8

0…8…16…24… 32 … 40 … 48

Or use multiplication:

Number	0	1	2	3	4	5	6	7	8
Number × 6	1	2	3	4	5	6	7	8	9

Number	0	1	2	3	4	5	6
Number × 8	2	3	4	5	6	7	8

Step 2: Look at either the addition lists or the multiplication tables. Which multiples of 6 are also multiples of 8?   X

Step 3: Which is the least of those numbers? X 8

So, X6 and X6 are the common multiples of 6 and 8, and Multi is their LCM.

Practice

1. Which of the numbers 17, 28, and 84 are multiples of 7?

   $\overset{2\,1\,7}{7\overline{)17}}$ $\qquad$ $\overset{2\,7\,9}{7\overline{)28}}$ $\qquad$ $\overset{4\,8\,7}{7\overline{)84}}$

   So, _____ and _____ are multiples of 7.

2. Complete the tables to find the first two common multiples of 3 and 7.

Number	0	1	2	3	4	5	6	7	8	9	10	11	12	13	14
Number × 3	0	3	6	9	12	15	18	21	24	27	30	33	36	39	42

Number	0	1	2	3	4	5	6
Number × 7	0	7	14	21	28	35	42

   The first two common multiples of 3 and 7 are _0_ and _0_ .

3. Find the first two common multiples of 4 and 10.

   Multiples of 4: 0, 4, 15, 18, 21, 24, 27, 30, 3~~7~~~~36~~

   Multiples of 10: 0, 10, 21, 28

   The first two common multiples of 4 and 10 are _18_ and _21_ .

4. Find the LCM of 6 and 14.

   Multiples of 6: 21, 24, 27, 30, 33, 36, 39

   Multiples of 14: 42, 14

   The LCM of 6 and 14 is _multiples_ .

Solve.

5. Is the sum of 3 and 7 a common multiple of 3 and 7? Yes

6. Is the product of 3 and 7 a common multiple of 3 and 7? Yes

7. What are the multiples of 1? 110, 10, 114, 115, 116, 117, 178, 119, 120, 121

8. What are the multiples of 0? 0, 02

9. What number is a multiple of every other number? LCM

   If one number is a multiple of another, what numbers are common multiples of both numbers?

2 $\qquad$ • TOPIC 6: Fractions, Mixed Numbers, and Percent Lesson 1

Problem Solving

1. Find the first two common multiples of 4 and 6.   *0* and *5*

2. Find the first two common multiples of 3 and 5.   *0* and *4*

3. Find the first two common multiples of 6 and 12.   *0* and *8*

4. Find the first two common multiples of 8 and 10.   *3* and *9*

5. Look for the pattern in the first two common multiples of each pair of numbers. Complete the table by predicting the next common multiple for each pair.

Numbers	First 2 Common Multiples	Pattern	Next Common Multiple
4 and 6	12 and 24	Add 12	*05*
3 and 5	*of*	*Add 8*	*12*
6 and 12	*06*	*Add 12*	*18*
8 and 10	*09*	*Add 3*	*17*

Check your predictions in problem 5 by finding the first five common multiples of each pair of numbers.

6. 4 and 6:   *10*

7. 3 and 5:   *8*

8. 6 and 12:   *18*

9. 8 and 10:   *18*

Solve.

10. Find the LCM of 9 and 15. *24*

11. Find the LCM of 7 and 12. *14*

12. How would you find the LCM of three numbers?
    Add the two numbers up
    Or you can subtract it

13. Find the LCM of 2, 3, and 4. *7*

14. Find the LCM of 4, 5, and 8. *17*

Connections

Write the letter of the matching expression.

1. $(3 \times 10) + 2$ `32`   **A** $3 \times 3 \times 3 \times 3$ ⁼

2. $(2 \times 100) + (5 \cdot \times 10)$ `250`   **B** $2 \times 2 \times 3 \times 7$ ⁼

3. $(8 \times 10) + 1$ `81`   **C** $2 \times 5 \times 5 \times 5$ ⁻

4. $(6 \times 100) + (2 \times 10) + 5$ `625`   **D** $2 \times 2 \times 2 \times 2 \times 2$ ⁻

5. $(8 \times 10) + 4$ `84`   **E** $5 \times 5 \times 5 \times 5$ ⁼

Write the letter of the matching expression.

6. $(9 \times 10) + 8$ `98`   **A** $2 \times 7 \times 7$ ⁼

7. $(3 \times 100) + (7 \times 10) + 5$ `375`   **B** 3×7 ⁼

8. $(1 \times 100) + (7 \times 10)$ `170`   **C** $3 \times 5 \times 5 \times 5$ ⁼

9. $(2 \times 10) + 1$ `21`   **D** $2 \times 3 \times 3 \times 7$ ⁼

10. $(1 \times 100) + (2 \times 10) + 6$ `126`   **E** $2 \times 5 \times 17$ ⁼

LANGUAGE OF MATHEMATICS

Solve.

11. I am a number between 20 and 30. The product of my digits is 14. What number am I?

12. I am a number between 35 and 50. The product of my digits is 12. What number am I?

13. I am a multiple of 6 and less than 100. The product of my digits is 36. What number am I?

14. I am a multiple of 4 and less than 50. The product of my digits is 16. What two numbers might I be?   and

15. I am a multiple of 9 and less than 100. The product of my digits is 20. What two numbers might I be?   and

16. I am a multiple of 7 and less than 100. The product of my digits is 18. What number am I?

Factors and Common Factors

REACHING MY GOAL
Find the greatest common factor of two whole numbers. (MA.A.5.2.1)

How did I do?

A. A **factor** is a positive whole number that divides into a number with no remainder.

Example 1

What are the factors of 72?

Step 1: Find each pair of positive whole numbers whose product is 72. Start with 1 and work up.

> **THINK**
> To determine if a number is a factor of 72, try dividing 72 by the number.

$1 \times 72 = 72$ $6 \times 12 = 72$

$2 \times 36 = 72$ $8 \times 9 = 72$

$3 \times 24 = 72$ $9 \times 8 = 72 \rightarrow 9 \times 8$ is a repeat of 8×9, so you can stop.

$4 \times 18 = 72$

Step 2: List the factors from the least to the greatest.

The factors of 72 are 1, 2, 3, 4, 6, 8, 9, 12, 18, 24, 36, and 72.

B. A factor of two or more numbers is a **common factor** of those numbers. The **greatest common factor**, or **GCF**, of two or more numbers is the common factor with the greatest value.

Example 2

What are the common factors of 48 and 64? What is the GCF of 48 and 64?

Step 1: Find the factors of each number.

$1 \times 48 = 48$ $1 \times 64 = 64$

$2 \times 24 = 48$ $2 \times 48 = 64$

$3 \times 12 = 48$ $3 \times 16 = 64$ IIII

$4 \times = 48$ $4 \times 8 = 64$

$5 \times 8 = 48$

Step 2: List the factors of each number.

Factors of 48: 1, 2, 3, 4, 5, 6, 7, 8, 9, and 10

Factors of 64: 1, 2, 3, 4, 5, 6, and 7

Step 3: Find the numbers that are factors of both 48 and 64.

4, 8, 7, 1, and 10

Step 4: Find the common factor with the greatest value. 10

So, the common factors of 48 and 64 are 4, 8, 7, 1, and 10, and the GCF is 10.

Practice

Use the numbers from the box at the right to answer questions 1–5.

9	33
10	35
15	40
30	45

1. Which of the numbers have 3 as a factor?

    _____ , _____ , _____ , _____ , and _____

2. Which of the numbers have 5 as a factor?

    _____ , _____ , _____ , _____ , _____ , and _____

3. Which of the numbers have 15 as a factor?

    _____ , _____ , and _____

4. Which of the numbers have 3 and 5 as a factor?

    _____ , _____ , and _____

5. What can you say about the numbers that have both 3 and 5 as factors and the numbers that have 15 as a factor?

    _____

Solve.

6. What are the factors of 40?

    _____

7. What are the factors of 17?

    _____

8. What are the factors of 98?

    _____

9. What are the common factors of 18 and 27? What is the GCF?

    Common factors _____   GCF _____

10. What are the common factors of 24 and 72? What is the GCF?

    Common factors _____   GCF _____

11. What are the common factors of 35 and 56? What is the GCF?

    Common factors _____   GCF _____

12. What are the common factors of 36 and 54? What is the GCF?

    Common factors _____   GCF _____

What number has only one factor?

Problem Solving

Use the information below to answer the questions on this page.

The AeroRug Company sells flying carpets. AeroRug's "48" family of carpets consists of carpets with an area of 48 square feet each. For example, the 4828 model is 8 ft long by 6 ft wide, so its area is 48 sq ft and its perimeter is 28 ft.

Hint: Create a table with all the possible carpet models in the "48" family. Write the dimensions, area, and perimeter of each carpet. You can also use the space on the page to draw a diagram of each carpet model.

1. What are the dimensions of the 4832 model?

2. What is the model number of the longest carpet in the "48" family?

3. How many models are in the "48" family?

4. Which carpet in the "48" family might be the hardest to sit on?

5. Which carpet in the "48" family is twice as long and half as wide as the 4832 model?

6. How many models are in AeroRug's "40" family of carpets?

7. AeroRug also has "84" and "88" families of carpets. Which of those families has more models?

8. AeroRug makes no carpets that are longer than 100 feet. Other than the "48" family, name a carpet family that has exactly 5 models.

   Hint: Each 5-model family has a carpet that is either 9 or 10 feet long.

Connections

Use the numbers from the box to write the divisor and the quotient for the problem.

47	5	11	17	12	3
4	2	7	10	25	9

1. ☐)44

2. ☐)170

3. ☐)125

4. ☐)63

5. ☐)36

6. ☐)94

ALGEBRA READINESS

Complete the table.

	Numbers	Product of Numbers	LCM of Numbers	GCF of Numbers	Product of LCM and GCF
	8 and 12	96	24	4	96
7.	5 and 10				
8.	6 and 14				
9.	9 and 15				
10.	12 and 30				

11. What pattern do you notice in the table?

LANGUAGE OF MATHEMATICS

Write the letter of the phrase that matches the number.

12. 18 ☐   A multiple of 7

13. 15 ☐   B GCF of 30 and 45

14. 8 ☐   C LCM of 6 and 9

15. 35 ☐   D factor of 56

Divisibility

A number is **divisible** by another number if they divide
with no remainder. So, a number is divisible by its
factors. You can test whether a number is divisible by certain numbers.

A. A number is divisible by 2 if its ones digit is either 0 or an even number.
A number is divisible by 4 if its last two digits read as a multiple of 4.

Example 1

Is 136 divisible by 2? Is it divisible by 4?

a. Is the ones digit either 0 or an even number? _____

So, 136 is divisible by 2.

b. What number is represented by the last two digits
of 136? _____
Is 36 a multiple of 4? _____

So, 136 is divisible by 4.

> **THINK**
> $9 \times 4 = 36$
> So, 36 is a multiple of 4.

B. A number is divisible by 3 if the sum of its digits is a multiple of 3.
A number is divisible by 9 if the sum of its digits is a multiple of 9.

Example 2

Is 534 divisible by 3? Is it divisible by 9?

a. What is the sum of the digits of 534? _____
Is 12 a multiple of 3? _____

So, 534 is divisible by 3.

b. Is 12 a multiple of 9? _____

So, 534 is not divisible by 9.

> **THINK**
> $4 \times 3 = 12$
> So, 12 is a multiple of 3.

C. A number is divisible by 6 if it is divisible by both 2 and 3.

Example 3

Is 396 divisible by 6?

Step 1: Is the ones digit of 396 either 0 or an even number? _____
You now know that 396 is divisible by 2.

Step 2: What is the sum of the digits of 396? _____
Is 18 a multiple of 3? _____
You now know that 396 is divisible by 3.

So, 396 is divisible by 6.

> **THINK**
> $6 \times 3 = 18$
> So, 18 is a multiple of 3.

Practice

A number is divisible by 5 if its ones digit is either 0 or 5.
A number is divisible by 10 if its ones digit is 0.

1. Is 210 divisible by 5? By 10?
   Is 235 divisible by 5? By 10?

   a. What is the ones digit of 210?

   So, 210 is divisible by both 5 and 10.

   b. What is the ones digit of 235?

   So, 235 is divisible by 5, but it is not divisible by 10.

Use the numbers from the box at the right to answer questions 2 and 3.

2. Which numbers are divisible by 2?

3. Which numbers are divisible by 4?

2	32
14	46
28	52
30	60

Use your answers to questions 2 and 3 to make general statements.

4. Write *sometimes*, *always*, or *never*.

   If a number is divisible by 2, then it is _____ divisible by 4.
   If a number is divisible by 4, then it is _____ divisible by 2.

Use the numbers from the box at the right to answer questions 5–7.

5. Which numbers are divisible by 3?

6. Which numbers are divisible by 6?

6	33
12	42
27	54
30	63

7. Which numbers are divisible by 9?

Use your answers to questions 5–7 to make general statements.

8. Write *sometimes*, *always*, or *never*.

   If a number is divisible by 3, then it is _____ divisible by 6.
   If a number is divisible by 9, then it is _____ divisible by 3.
   If a number is divisible by 9, then it is _____ divisible by 6.

Problem Solving

Solve.

1. I am a number between 1,300 and 1,345. I am divisible by both 5 and 9. What number am I? ▨

2. I am a number between 1,415 and 1,455. I am divisible by both 6 and 10. What number am I? ▨

3. I am a number between 2,010 and 2,030. I am divisible by both 4 and 5. What number am I? ▨

4. I am a number between 2,305 and 2,325. I am divisible by 3, 4, and 6. What number am I? ▨

5. I am a number between 4,250 and 4,350. I am divisible by 5, 6, and 9. What number am I? ▨

Write the number from the box that matches the sentence.

6. I am divisible by 2, 3, and 5. ▨

7. I am divisible by 4, but not by 6. ▨

8. I am divisible by 3, 5, and 9. ▨

9. I am divisible by 6 and 9, but not by 4. ▨

10. I am divisible by 3 and 4. ▨

```
234   324
236   330
   405
```

Use the clues to write the missing digits of the number.

11. I am a number less than 850. I am divisible by 5 and 9.   8 __ __

12. I am a number between 910 and 970. I am divisible by 4 and 9.   9 __ __

13. I am a number greater than 300. I am divisible by 3, 4, and 5.   3 __ __

14. I am a number less than 500. I am divisible by 2, 5, and 9.   4 __ __

What number is divisible by every number?

Connections

You can use the table below to help you decide whether a number is divisible by another number.

DIVISIBILITY RULES	
Number	Divisible by
The ones digit is 0 or an even number.	2
The sum of the digits is a multiple of 3.	3
The tens and ones digits form a multiple of 4.	4
The ones digit is either 0 or 5.	5
The number is divisible by both 2 and 3.	6
The sum of the digits is a multiple of 9.	9
The ones digit is 0.	10

Decide whether the first number in each pair is divisible by the second number. If so, find the quotient.

1. 903 and 5

2. 645 and 3

3. 568 and 4

4. 837 and 9

5. 824 and 6

6. 738 and 9

ALGEBRA READINESS

Find the greatest number that is a factor of every number in the set.

7.
183	60	27	150

8.
1,000	400	800	9,995

9.
12	30	64	102

Prime and Composite Numbers

REACHING MY GOAL
Express a number as a product
of its prime factors. (MA.A.5.2.1)

How did I do?

A. Some numbers have more factors than other numbers.

- Numbers that have only 2 factors are called **prime numbers**. A prime number has only itself and 1 as factors. 47 is a prime number; its only factors are 1 and 47.

- Numbers that have 3 or more factors are called **composite numbers**. 46 is a composite number; its factors are 1, 2, 23, and 46.

- 1 is the only positive whole number with just one factor. Since 1 has only one factor, 1 is neither prime nor composite.

Example 1

Is 27 prime or composite? Is 29 prime or composite?

Find the factors of each number.

a. factors of 27: ⬚⬚⬚⬚⬚⬚   **b.** factors of 29: ⬚⬚⬚⬚⬚⬚

So, ⬚⬚⬚ is a prime number and ⬚⬚⬚ is a composite number.

B. Any whole number greater than 1 can be written as a product of prime numbers. This is called the **prime factorization** of the number. You can use a **factor tree** to find the prime factorization of a number.

Example 2

What is the prime factorization of 24?

Step 1: Write a pair of factors of 24. You can start with any pair.

$$24$$
$$3 \times 8$$

Step 2: Write a pair of factors for each composite factor.

$$24$$
$$3 \times 8$$
$$3 \times 2 \times 4$$

> **THINK**
> 3 is prime, but 8 is composite. I can find factors of 8.

Step 3: Continue factoring until all the factors are prime numbers.

$$24$$
$$3 \times 8$$
$$3 \times 2 \times 4$$
$$3 \times 2 \times 2 \times 2$$

> **THINK**
> 2 is prime, but 4 is composite. I can find factors of 4.

So, listing the prime factors from least to greatest, the prime factorization of 24 is $2 \times 2 \times 2 \times 3$.

Practice

For problems 1–6, write whether the number is prime or composite. Use rules of divisibility to help you.

1. 33 ▢
2. 23 ▢
3. 4 ▢
4. 19 ▢
5. 108 ▢
6. 87 ▢

7. What is the prime factorization of 72?

   a. Write a pair of factors of 72.

   72   72
   / \   / \
   6 × ▢   or   ▢ × 9

   b. Write a pair of factors for each composite factor.

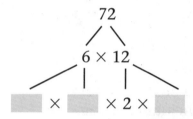   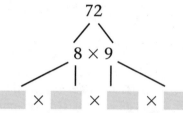

   72   72
   / \   / \
   6 × 12   or   8 × 9
   / | | \   / | | \
   ▢ × ▢ × 2 × ▢   ▢ × ▢ × ▢ × ▢

   c. Continue factoring until all the factors are prime numbers.

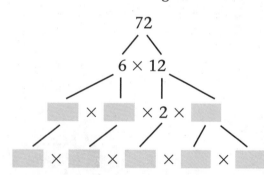   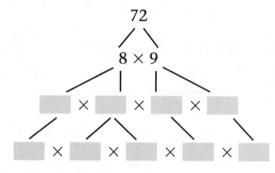

   The prime factorization of 72 is ▢.

8. Use the factor trees in problem 7 to make a general statement about prime factors.

   > No matter how you factor a number, you get ▢ set of prime factors.

9. Find the prime factorization of 84. ▢

10. Find the prime factorization of 175. ▢

11. Find the prime factorization of 195. ▢

12. Find the prime factorization of 462. ▢

Problem Solving

1. Help Hector and Helen find the prime factorization of 420.

Hector's Way	Helen's Way

Hector's Way

a. I check if 2 is a factor. If it is, I factor 2 out as many times as I can.

$420 = 2 \times 210$

$210 = 2 \times 105$
105 is not divisible by 2.

b. Then I check 3 as a factor.

$105 = 3 \times 35$
35 is not divisible by 3.

c. I keep trying greater prime numbers until all the factors are prime numbers.

$35 = 5 \times 7$
7 is a prime number.

So, 420 = ▨▨▨▨▨ .

Helen's Way

a. I use divisibility tests to find a factor.

Think: The sum of the digits of 420 is 6, so 420 is divisible by 3.

b. Then I use a factor tree.

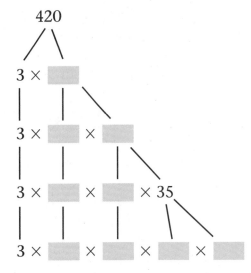

So, 420 = ▨▨▨▨▨ .

Use both Hector's and Helen's ways to find the prime factorization of the number.

2. 693 → ▨▨▨▨▨

3. 294 → ▨▨▨▨▨

4. 375 → ▨▨▨▨▨

5. 780 → ▨▨▨▨▨

6. Which way was easier for you to find the prime factorization? Why?

Can a 4-digit number have fewer factors than a 1-digit number? Explain.

Connections

Find the missing measures of the prism. Use prime factors to help you.

1.

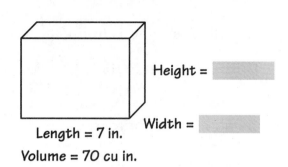

Height =
Width =
Length = 7 in.
Volume = 70 cu in.

2.

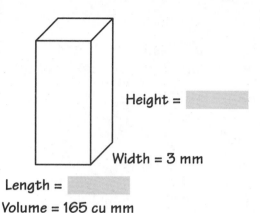

Height =
Width = 3 mm
Length =
Volume = 165 cu mm

3.

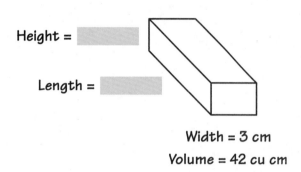

Height =
Length =
Width = 3 cm
Volume = 42 cu cm

4.

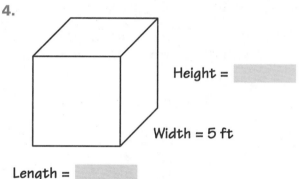

Height =
Width = 5 ft
Length =
Volume = 245 cu ft

5.

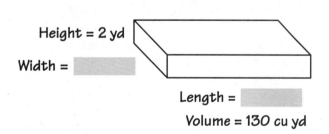

Height = 2 yd
Width =
Length =
Volume = 130 cu yd

6.

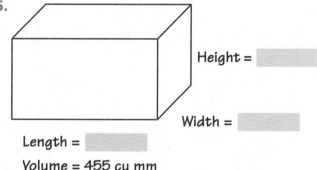

Height =
Width =
Length =
Volume = 455 cu mm

LANGUAGE OF MATHEMATICS

Write the letter of the expression or set of numbers that best matches each phrase.

7. Factors of 42

8. Prime factors of 42

9. Prime factorization of 42

A 2, 3, 7

B 1, 2, 3, 7

C 1, 2, 3, 6, 7, 14, 21, 42

D 2 × 3 × 7

Patterns with Square Numbers

A. The product of a number multiplied by itself is a **square number** or **perfect square**. If you made an array of objects to show the product of 6 × 6, with 6 rows of 6 objects, you would make a square pattern like the one shown at the right. That is why numbers such as 4 (or 2 × 2), 9 (or 3 × 3), and 36 (or 6 × 6) are called perfect squares.

Example 1

Complete the table of square numbers.

Number	Number Times Itself	Square of Number
1	1 × 1	1
2	2 × 2	4
3	3 × 3	9
4	4 × 4	
5	5 × 5	
6	6 × 6	36
7	7 × 7	
8	8 × 8	
9	9 × 9	
10	10 × 10	
11	11 × 11	
12	12 × 12	

B. You can find the next perfect square by adding a new column and a new row to an array that is already a square.

Example 2

Predict how many dots you need to add to a 4 × 4 array to make a 5 × 5 array.

= 1 × 1   = 2 × 2   = 3 × 3   = 4 × 4

3 dots added   5 dots added   7 dots added

Find the pattern in the number of dots added to each new array.

So, you need to add _____ dots to a 4 × 4 array to make a 5 × 5 array.

Practice

1. Complete the table.

Sum of Consecutive Odd Numbers	Total	Square of Which Number?
1	1	1
1 + 3	4	2
1 + 3 + 5	9	3
1 + 3 + 5 + 7		
1 + 3 + 5 + 7 + 9		
1 + 3 + 5 + 7 + 9 + 11		
1 + 3 + 5 + 7 + 9 + 11 + 13		
1 + 3 + 5 + 7 + 9 + 11 + 13 + 15		
1 + 3 + 5 + 7 + 9 + 11 + 13 + 15 + 17		
1 + 3 + 5 + 7 + 9 + 11 + 13 + 15 + 17 + 19		
1 + 3 + 5 + 7 + 9 + 11 + 13 + 15 + 17 + 19 + 21		
1 + 3 + 5 + 7 + 9 + 11 + 13 + 15 + 17 + 19 + 21 + 23		

2. Make a general statement about the sequence of perfect squares.

> You can find the sequence of perfect squares by adding on consecutive _____ numbers.

3. Complete the table.

Number (n)	Number Times Itself (n × n)	(Number + 1) × (Number − 1) (n + 1) × (n − 1)
3	3 × 3 = 9	4 × 2 = 8
6	6 × 6 = 36	7 × 5 = 35
8	8 × 8 = 64	9 × 7 = 63
10		
11		

4. Make a general statement about the pattern shown in the table.

> The square of a number is _____ more than the product of that number plus one and that number minus one.

Use the pattern from problem 4 to find the product.

5. $61 \times 59 = ($ _____ $\times$ _____ $) - 1 \rightarrow$ _____

6. $81 \times 79 = ($ _____ $\times$ _____ $) - 1 \rightarrow$ _____

7. $101 \times 99 = ($ _____ $\times$ _____ $) - 1 \rightarrow$ _____

Problem Solving

1. Complete the table of square numbers.

11 × 11 = 121	21 × 21 = 441	31 × 31 =
12 × 12 = 144	22 × 22 = 484	32 × 32 =
13 × 13 = 169	23 × 23 = 529	33 × 33 =
14 × 14 = 196	24 × 24 =	34 × 34 = 1,156
15 × 15 = 225	25 × 25 =	35 × 35 = 1,225
16 × 16 =	26 × 26 = 676	36 × 36 = 1,296
17 × 17 =	27 × 27 = 729	37 × 37 = 1,369
18 × 18 = 324	28 × 28 =	38 × 38 =
19 × 19 =	29 × 29 =	39 × 39 = 1,521
20 × 20 =	30 × 30 =	40 × 40 =

Use the table in problem 1 to make general statements about square numbers.

2. If the square of a number ends in 1, the number ends in   .

3. If the square of a number ends in 4, the number ends in   .

4. If the square of a number ends in 9, the number ends in   .

5. If the square of a number ends in 6, the number ends in   .

6. If the square of a number ends in 5, the number ends in   .

7. If the square of a number ends in 0, the number ends in   .

Circle the letter of the correct answer.

8. 9,025 is the square of what number?

   F 93   H 95

   G 94   I 96

9. 7,744 is the square of what number?

   A 82   C 86

   B 84   D 88

10. 2,809 is the square of what number?

   F 51   H 55

   G 53   I 57

11. 12,996 is the square of what number?

   A 114   C 124

   B 116   D 126

Connections

Find the area of the square and of the rectangle.

1. 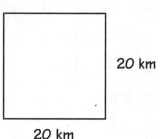 20 km, 20 km

   Area = _____

   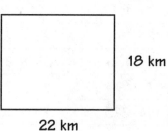 18 km, 22 km

   Area = _____

2. 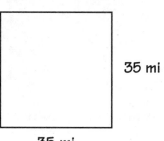 35 mi, 35 mi

   Area = _____

   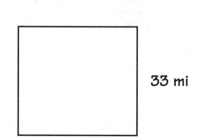 33 mi, 37 mi

   Area = _____

3. 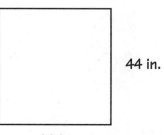 44 in., 44 in.

   Area = _____

   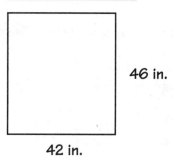 46 in., 42 in.

   Area = _____

4. 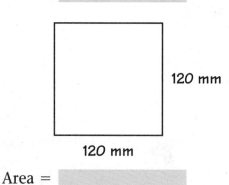 120 mm, 120 mm

   Area = _____

   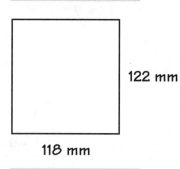 122 mm, 118 mm

   Area = _____

Make a general statement about the pattern shown in problems 1–4.

5. The square of a number is _____ more than the product of that number plus two and that number minus two.

Set Comparisons

REACHING MY GOAL
Compare sets by writing ratios and fractions. (MA.A.1.2.3)

How did I do?

A. You can write a **ratio** to compare the quantities of two sets. You can also write a **fraction** to compare two sets.

The ratio of the set of striped gourds to the set of all gourds is 3:10 (read 3 to 10), which you can write as the fraction $\frac{3}{10}$.

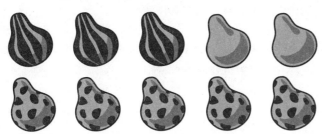

striped gourds → $\frac{3}{10}$ ← The **numerator** is the first number you're considering.
all gourds →   ← The **denominator** is the second number you're considering.

Example 1

What fraction of the gourds are spotted?

There are 5 spotted gourds.

There are ⬜ gourds altogether.

So, $\frac{5}{}$ of the gourds are spotted.

B. You can also use ratios to compare one part of a set to another part of the set, or to compare the whole set to a part.

Example 2

Compare the number of striped gourds to the number of unstriped gourds.

There are 3 striped gourds.

There are ⬜ unstriped gourds.

So, the ratio of striped gourds to unstriped gourds is 3: ⬜ , or $\frac{3}{}$.

Example 3

Compare the set of all gourds to the set of plain gourds.

There are 10 gourds altogether.

There are ⬜ plain gourds.

So, the ratio of all gourds to plain gourds is 10: ⬜ , or $\frac{10}{}$.

Practice

Use the set of sea stars to answer questions 1–6.

1. What fraction of the sea stars have spots?

   Write the number of spotted sea stars: 4.
   Write the number of all sea stars: [ ].

   So, $\dfrac{4}{}$ of the sea stars have spots.

2. Compare the gray sea stars to the pink sea stars.

   There are [ ] gray sea stars.
   There are [ ] pink sea stars.

   So, the ratio of gray sea stars to pink sea stars is [ ] : [ ].

   You can write this ratio as the fraction $\dfrac{}{}$.

3. What fraction of the sea stars are gray?

4. What is the ratio of all sea stars to spotted sea stars?

5. Write a ratio to compare the pink sea stars to the spotted sea stars.

6. What fraction of the sea stars are pink?

Solve.

7. Last week, Mr. Samuels ate 11 sandwiches. Eight of them were peanut butter and jelly sandwiches. What fraction of the total sandwiches were peanut butter and jelly sandwiches?

8. Ms. Reyna bought 7 fish for her aquarium. Four of the fish were guppies, and 3 were tetras. Write a ratio comparing the guppies to the tetras.

9. In Luis's building, 15 people live on the first floor, 12 people live on the second floor, and 9 people live on the third floor. What fraction of the people in Luis's building live on the first floor?

10. Sue found 6 carrots, 4 tomatoes, and 5 cucumbers in her salad. What fraction of the vegetables were tomatoes? What is the ratio of carrots to cucumbers?

Problem Solving

Amanda has the same number of coins in each of her two pockets. The coins are pennies, nickels, dimes, and quarters. **Follow the clues to complete the diagram showing the coins in Amanda's pockets. Answering the questions will help you.**

Clues

- The ratio of pennies to nickels in her left pocket is $\frac{3}{2}$.
- $\frac{3}{10}$ of the coins in her right pocket are quarters.
- She has the same number of dimes in each pocket.
- She has 7 quarters in all.
- The coins in her right pocket total $1.07.

Think: The ratio of pennies to nickels in Amanda's left pocket is $\frac{3}{2}$. The number of pennies is 3, and the number of nickels is _____. I should draw 3 pennies and _____ nickels in the left pocket.

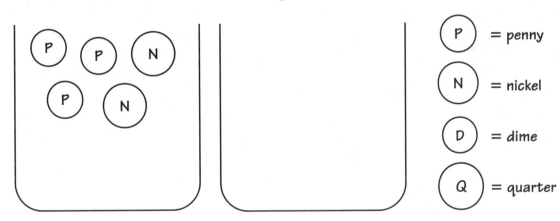

Left Pocket   **Right Pocket**

P = penny
N = nickel
D = dime
Q = quarter

1. How many coins are in Amanda's right pocket? _____

2. How many quarters are in her left pocket? _____

3. How many dimes are in each pocket? _____

4. What is the ratio of pennies to nickels in her right pocket? _____

5. How much money does she have altogether? _____

6. What fraction of all the coins are pennies? _____

Connections

Mary put food in her frog's tank and kept a daily record of what it ate.
Use the chart to answer questions 1–4.

1. What is the ratio of mealworms eaten to crickets eaten for the three days?

Australian Dumpy Frog's Diet			
Food	Monday	Tuesday	Wednesday
Mealworms	||||	|||	|||| ||||
Crickets	|||	||||	||

2. What fraction of the total number of crickets did the frog eat on Monday?

3. What fraction of the total number of mealworms did the frog eat on Wednesday?

4. Compare the number of mealworms eaten on Monday to the number of mealworms eaten on Tuesday.

Use the graph to answer questions 5–8.

5. What fraction of Noera's books are westerns?

6. What is the ratio of mysteries to natural histories in her library?

7. What fraction of the books are biographies?

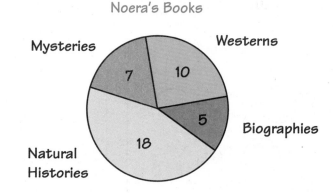

Noera's Books

Mysteries 7 — Westerns 10 — Biographies 5 — Natural Histories 18

8. Compare the number of all books to the number of natural histories.

ALGEBRA READINESS

9. George puts 5 muffins in the refrigerator. He tells his brother that $\frac{4}{5}$ of them are corn muffins, and that $\frac{3}{5}$ of them have blueberries. If George is telling the truth, what is the greatest number of corn muffins with blueberries that can be in the refrigerator? The least number?

10. George has 10 marbles in his pocket. The ratio of cat's-eye marbles to clear marbles is $\frac{5}{5}$. The ratio of blue marbles to green marbles is $\frac{4}{6}$. What is the greatest number of green cat's-eye marbles he can have in his pocket? The least number?

Parts of a Whole

REACHING MY GOAL
Use fractions to show parts of wholes, and write the fractions as decimals and percents. (MA.A.1.2.4)

How did I do?

A. You can use a fraction to show a part of a whole. The whole must be separated into equal parts.

Example 1

What fraction of the rectangle is gray?

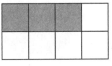

There are 3 gray parts.

There are ▨ parts altogether.

$\dfrac{3}{8}$ ← The **numerator** is the number of equal parts you're considering.

← The **denominator** is the number of equal parts in the whole.

So, $\dfrac{3}{}$ of the rectangle is gray.

B. When a whole is separated into tenths, hundredths, or thousandths, you can write a fraction as a decimal.

$\dfrac{7}{10}$ ← The whole is separated into tenths, so write 0.7.

↑ tenths place

$\dfrac{38}{100}$ ← The whole is separated into ▨, so write 0.38.

↑ hundredths place

$\dfrac{125}{1000}$ ← The whole is separated into ▨, so write 0.125.

↑ thousandths place

C. When a whole is separated into hundredths, you can write a fraction as a percent. The word **percent** means *per hundred*.

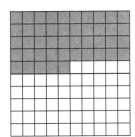

→ $\dfrac{45}{100}$ → 0.45 → 45%

↑ percent symbol

Example 2

Mel has 100 CDs in his music collection. Twenty-seven of the CDs are rock 'n' roll. **What percent of Mel's collection is rock 'n' roll?**

Mel's music collection has 100 equal parts.

$\dfrac{}{100}$ of his collection is rock 'n' roll.

So, ▨ of Mel's collection is rock 'n' roll.

Practice

Write the fraction of the figure that is shaded. If the figure has tenths or hundredths, write the decimal as well. If the figure has hundredths, write the fraction, the decimal, and the percent.

1.

$\dfrac{1}{}$

2.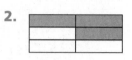

$\dfrac{}{6}$

3.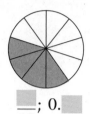

$\dfrac{}{10}$; 0.◻

4.

_____

5.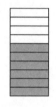

_____

6.

_____

7.

_____

8.

_____

9.

_____

10.

_____

11.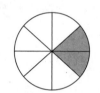

_____

12.

_____

Solve.

13. Mrs. Ross has 3 black hens, 5 red hens, and 2 yellow hens.

    What fraction of the hens are yellow? _____

    Which group of hens makes up 0.3 of the total? _____

14. Twenty-four students are playing soccer, 17 are playing softball, 49 are playing basketball, and 10 are playing volleyball.

    What fraction of the students are playing soccer? _____

    What percent of the students are playing basketball? _____

15. Mustafa bought 52 apples, 33 figs, and 15 apricots.

    What fraction of the fruits are apricots? _____

    Which group of fruit makes up 0.52 of the total? _____

    What percent of the fruits are figs? _____

Problem Solving

Complete the graph and table, and then answer the questions.

Favorite Ice-Cream Flavors of Students in Mr. O'Neill's Class

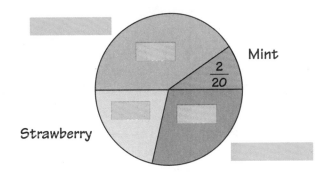

Flavor	Students
Chocolate	∫⧗ III
Mint	
	IIII
Vanilla	

1. How many students are in the class?

2. Which flavor is the most popular?

3. What fraction of the students prefer vanilla?

Colors of Bicycles at Roosevelt Elementary School

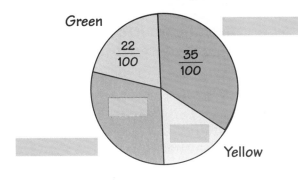

Color	Bicycles
Blue	
Green	
Red	35
	16

4. How many bicycles are at the school?

5. Which group of bicycles make up 0.27 of the total?

6. What percent of the bicycles are yellow?

7. Which color of bicycle is the least common?

When the denominator of a fraction is double the size of the numerator, the fraction is equivalent to $\frac{1}{2}$. What percent is equivalent to $\frac{1}{2}$?

Connections

Use the map to solve problems 1–8.

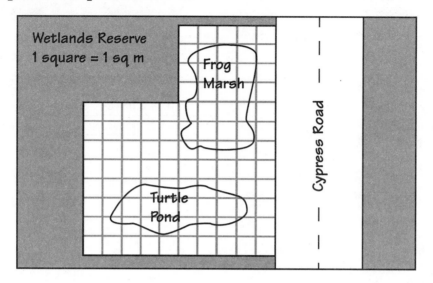

1. Estimate the area of Turtle Pond.

2. Estimate the area of Frog Marsh.

3. Estimate the fraction of the Reserve's area that is covered by Frog Marsh.

4. Estimate the percent of the Reserve's area that is covered by Turtle Pond.

5. Compare the estimated area of Frog Marsh to the estimated area of Turtle Pond.

6. Estimate the percent of the Reserve's area that is covered by water.

7. What fraction of the Reserve's perimeter is along Cypress Road?

8. Estimate the fraction of the Reserve's *water* area that is made up by Turtle Pond.

ALGEBRA READINESS

Find the tenth term in each sequence.

9. $\frac{3}{50}, \frac{8}{50}, \frac{13}{50} \cdots$

10. 20%, 24%, 28% . . .

11. 0.1, 0.8, 0.15 . . .

12. $\frac{74}{100}, \frac{72}{100}, \frac{70}{100} \cdots$

13. 85%, 80%, 75% . . .

14. 1.17, 1.27, 1.37 . . .

Equivalent Fractions

A. Two fractions that represent equal numbers are called **equivalent fractions**.

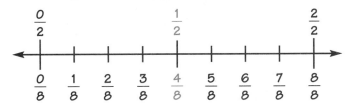

The fractions $\frac{1}{2}$ and $\frac{4}{8}$ are the same point on the number line, so they are equivalent.

B. You can create equivalent fractions. Multiply—or divide—the numerator and the denominator of a given fraction by the same number.

Example 1

Find two fractions that are equivalent to $\frac{6}{10}$.

Multiply. $\quad \frac{6 \times 3}{10 \times 3} = \frac{18}{30}$ $\qquad$ Divide. $\quad \frac{6 \div 2}{10 \div 2} = \frac{3}{5}$

The fractions $\frac{6}{10}$, $\frac{18}{30}$, and $\frac{3}{5}$ are equivalent.

C. To test whether fractions are equivalent, rename them as fractions that have the same denominator.

Example 2

Are $\frac{4}{6}$ and $\frac{6}{9}$ equivalent?

Step 1: Find a common multiple of the denominators.

$$6 \quad 12 \quad 18 \quad 24 \dots$$

$$9 \quad 18 \quad 27 \dots$$

<u>   </u> is a common multiple of the denominators.

Step 2: Rename each fraction as a fraction with a denominator of 18.

$$\frac{4 \times 3}{6 \times 3} = \frac{\rule{0.5cm}{0.3cm}}{18} \qquad\qquad \frac{6 \times \rule{0.4cm}{0.3cm}}{9 \times \rule{0.4cm}{0.3cm}} = \frac{\rule{0.5cm}{0.3cm}}{18}$$

<u>   </u>, $\frac{4}{6}$ and $\frac{6}{9}$ <u>   </u> equivalent.

> Could you use division to show that $\frac{4}{6}$ and $\frac{6}{9}$ are equivalent?

Practice

1. What fraction of the rectangle is gray?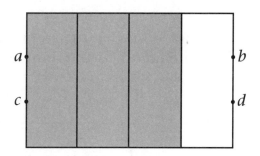

   Draw a line from *a* to *b*. Draw a line from *c* to *d*.

   Now there are 9 equal gray parts, and the rectangle is separated into [   ] equal parts.

   What fraction equivalent to $\frac{3}{4}$ did you create by drawing the lines? [   ]

Write the fraction of the rectangle that is gray. Draw lines between the points to separate the rectangle into equal parts. Write the equivalent fraction that you created.

2.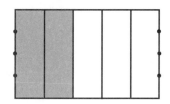

   fraction: [   ]

   equivalent fraction: [   ]

3.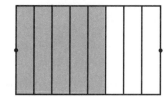

   fraction: [   ]

   equivalent fraction: [   ]

Find the numerator or denominator to make an equivalent fraction.

4. $\frac{5}{6} = \frac{\Box}{12}$

5. $\frac{9}{21} = \frac{3}{\Box}$

6. $\frac{2}{10} = \frac{20}{\Box}$

7. $\frac{4}{16} = \frac{\Box}{4}$

Choose numbers from the box to write two equivalent fractions.

8. $\frac{4}{6} = \frac{\Box}{\Box} = \frac{\Box}{\Box}$

2		18
	10	12
16		3

9. $\frac{8}{20} = \frac{\Box}{\Box} = \frac{\Box}{\Box}$

32		5
		40
2	16	4

Write *yes* or *no*.

10. Are $\frac{9}{12}$ and $\frac{6}{9}$ equivalent? [   ]

11. Are $\frac{4}{8}$ and $\frac{5}{10}$ equivalent? [   ]

12. Are $\frac{2}{8}$ and $\frac{3}{12}$ equivalent? [   ]

13. Are $\frac{2}{7}$ and $\frac{1}{4}$ equivalent? [   ]

14. Are $\frac{4}{6}$ and $\frac{10}{15}$ equivalent? [   ]

15. Are $\frac{6}{10}$ and $\frac{3}{4}$ equivalent? [   ]

Problem Solving

A hardware store received its July shipment of paint. **Complete the circle graph and the pictograph, and solve the problems.**

July Paint Shipment: 240 Gallons

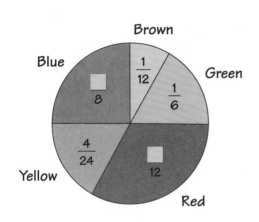

= 10 gallons

1. How many gallons of green paint were in the shipment?

   The total shipment was ⬜ gallons.

   The fraction of paint that was green was $\frac{⬜}{⬜}$.

   Think: I can calculate an equivalent fraction.

   $$\frac{1}{6} = \frac{?}{240} \quad \begin{array}{l} \leftarrow \text{gallons of green paint} \\ \leftarrow \text{gallons in total shipment} \end{array}$$

   $$\frac{1 \times ⬜}{6 \times ⬜} = \frac{⬜}{240}$$

   So, ⬜ gallons of green paint were in the shipment.
   In the pictograph, 1 can is 10 gallons, so draw ⬜ cans.

2. Which two colors of paint were the same quantity?

3. Which two colors of paint were equivalent fractions of the shipment?

4. Write two colors of paint that together made up half the shipment.

5. Write three colors of paint that together made up half the shipment.

6. The June paint shipment was smaller. The ratio of June paint to July paint was 3:4. How many gallons of paint were received in June?

Connections

Write the letter of the equivalent fraction of each decimal.

1. 0.35 _____
2. 0.8 _____
3. 0.9 _____
4. 0.36 _____
5. 0.55 _____
6. 0.06 _____
7. 0.75 _____
8. 0.48 _____

A $\dfrac{9}{25}$

B $\dfrac{9}{10}$

C $\dfrac{7}{20}$

D $\dfrac{12}{25}$

E $\dfrac{3}{4}$

F $\dfrac{11}{20}$

G $\dfrac{4}{5}$

H $\dfrac{3}{50}$

ALGEBRA READINESS

Circle the letter of the correct answer.

9.

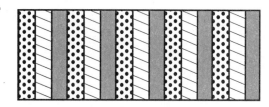

What fraction of the rectangle is *not* striped?

A $\dfrac{1}{3}$ **C** $\dfrac{2}{3}$

B $\dfrac{5}{15}$ **D** $\dfrac{8}{15}$

10.

What fraction of the marbles are *not* red?

F $\dfrac{8}{20}$ **H** $\dfrac{2}{5}$

G $\dfrac{3}{5}$ **I** $\dfrac{3}{10}$

11. Mrs. Bell has 17 coins from Egypt, 18 coins from England, and 15 coins from Ecuador. What fraction of the coins are *not* from Ecuador?

A $\dfrac{7}{10}$ **C** $\dfrac{9}{25}$

B $\dfrac{3}{10}$ **D** $\dfrac{7}{25}$

12. A cook purchased 8 lb of butter, 13 lb of margarine, 5 lb of lard, and 4 lb of fat. What fraction of the pounds purchased were *not* lard?

F $\dfrac{7}{10}$ **H** $\dfrac{2}{3}$

G $\dfrac{1}{5}$ **I** $\dfrac{5}{6}$

Renaming Fractions and Mixed Numbers

REACHING MY GOAL
Write fractions greater than 1 as mixed numbers, and write mixed numbers as fractions. (MA.A.1.2.4)

How did I do?

A fraction greater than 1 is equivalent to a mixed number.

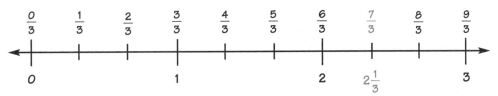

The fraction $\frac{7}{3}$ and the mixed number $2\frac{1}{3}$ are the same point on the number line, so they are equivalent.

A. You can rename a mixed number as a fraction. You can rename a fraction greater than 1 as a mixed number.

Example 1

Rename $4\frac{2}{3}$ as a fraction.

Write the mixed number as a sum.

Write the whole-number addend as a fraction.

Add the numerators.

$$4\frac{2}{3} = 4 + \frac{2}{3}$$
$$= \frac{12}{3} + \frac{2}{3}$$
$$= \frac{14}{3}$$

> **THINK**
> How many thirds are in 4?

Example 2

Rename $\frac{17}{4}$ as a mixed number.

Separate the fraction into two parts.

Write the first addend as a whole number.

$$\frac{17}{4} = \frac{16}{4} + \frac{1}{4}$$
$$= \boxed{} + \frac{1}{4}$$
$$= \boxed{}\frac{1}{4}$$

> **THINK**
> What is the greatest multiple of 4 that is less than 17?
> 4 8 12 16 . . .

B. To rename a fraction greater than 1 in simplest form, write it as a mixed number that cannot be renamed with a lower denominator.

Example 3

Write $\frac{28}{8}$ in simplest form.

$$\frac{28}{8} = \frac{\boxed{}}{8} + \frac{4}{8}$$

$$= 3\frac{4}{8} \qquad \textbf{Think:} \text{ I can rename } \frac{4}{8} \text{ as a fraction with a lower denominator.}$$

$$= 3\frac{\boxed{}}{2}$$

Practice

Rename the mixed number as a fraction.

1. $2\frac{1}{5}$ $\rightarrow$ $2 + \frac{1}{5}$ $\rightarrow$ $\frac{\boxed{}}{5} + \frac{1}{5}$ $\rightarrow$ $\frac{\boxed{}}{5}$

2. $4\frac{5}{6}$ $\frac{\boxed{}}{\boxed{}}$

3. $1\frac{15}{16}$ $\frac{\boxed{}}{\boxed{}}$

4. $8\frac{1}{2}$ $\frac{\boxed{}}{\boxed{}}$

5. $3\frac{4}{7}$ $\frac{\boxed{}}{\boxed{}}$

Rename the fraction as a whole number or a mixed number.

6. $\frac{20}{3}$ $\rightarrow$ $\frac{\boxed{}}{3} + \frac{2}{3}$ $\rightarrow$ $\boxed{}\frac{2}{3}$

7. $\frac{7}{4}$ $\boxed{}$

8. $\frac{32}{8}$ $\boxed{}$

9. $\frac{47}{9}$ $\boxed{}$

10. $\frac{18}{5}$ $\boxed{}$

Write the fraction in simplest form.

11. $\frac{22}{6}$ $\boxed{}$

12. $\frac{38}{4}$ $\boxed{}$

13. $\frac{26}{12}$ $\boxed{}$

14. $\frac{30}{16}$ $\boxed{}$

Test whether the numbers in each pair are equivalent by writing them in simplest form. Circle *equivalent* or *not equivalent*.

15. $2\frac{6}{9}, \frac{16}{6}$

$2\frac{6}{9} = 2\frac{\boxed{}}{\boxed{}}$

$\frac{16}{6} = \boxed{}\frac{\boxed{}}{3}$

equivalent   not equivalent

16. $\frac{46}{8}, 5\frac{9}{12}$

$\frac{46}{8} = \boxed{}$

$5\frac{9}{12} = \boxed{}$

equivalent   not equivalent

17. $1\frac{10}{16}, \frac{24}{16}$

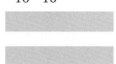

equivalent   not equivalent

18. $\frac{82}{8}, 11\frac{5}{20}$

equivalent   not equivalent

Problem Solving

An artist made 25 gold-leaf figures. The wind blew some away. The wind did not blow away any triangles. **Use the table to find which figures are missing. Draw the missing figures, complete the table, and solve the problems.**

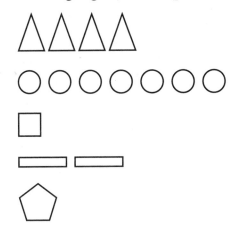

Ratios			
○	to △	=	$\frac{5}{2}$
△	to □	=	$\frac{2}{1}$
▭	to □	=	$\frac{3}{1}$
⬠	to ▭	=	$\frac{}{2}$

1. How many circles did the wind blow away?

   The ratio of circles to triangles is ▢ —.

   Think: I can calculate an equivalent ratio.

   $\frac{5}{2} = \frac{}{4}$ ← Circles
             ← Triangles

   Subtract the number of circles remaining from the total number of circles.

   ▢ − 7 = ▢

   So, the wind blew away ▢ circles.

2. How many squares did the wind blow away?

   Think: I can use the ratio of triangles to squares because I know the quantity of triangles.

   ▢

3. In simplest form, the ratio of ▢ to ▢ is 3:5.

4. In simplest form, what is the ratio of remaining figures to missing figures?

   ▢

5. In simplest form, what is the ratio of missing rectangles to all missing figures?

   ▢

What is an equivalent ratio of $2\frac{1}{2}$ to 1?

• TOPIC 6: Fractions, Mixed Numbers, and Percent Lesson 9

35

Connections

Write the direction the person faces after making the turns. Then write a whole number or mixed number to show how many full turns the person has made. You can use the compass to help you solve the problems.

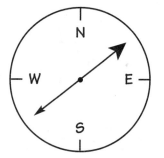

1. Jeremy is driving north. He makes 9 right turns in a row. Each turn is a quarter-turn. _____

2. Ellen is walking west. She made 7 turns in a row. Each turn is a half-turn. _____

3. Alan is riding his unicycle south. He makes 22 quarter-turns to the right. _____

4. Olivia is swimming east. She makes 12 half-turns. _____

5. A gardener is mowing a lawn. He is mowing south. He makes 11 quarter-turns to the left. _____

Circle the letter of the correct answer.

6. How many $\frac{1}{4}$-cup glasses can be filled with $3\frac{3}{4}$ cups of olive oil?

   F 9   **H** 13

   G 11   **I** 15

7. How many $\frac{1}{2}$-gallon jugs can be filled with 25 gal of juice?

   A $12\frac{1}{2}$ **C** 50

   B 13   **D** $50\frac{1}{2}$

8. How many $\frac{1}{3}$-cup bowls can be filled with $15\frac{2}{3}$ cups of pudding?

   F 33   **H** 48

   G 47   **I** 60

9. How many $\frac{1}{8}$-cup dishes can be filled with $4\frac{1}{2}$ cups of hot sauce?

   A 9   **C** 36

   B 12   **D** 38

Compare. Write <, >, or =.

10. $3\frac{1}{9}$ ⬭ $\frac{10}{3}$

11. $6\frac{1}{4}$ ⬭ $\frac{100}{16}$

12. $\frac{20}{16}$ ⬭ $1\frac{1}{8}$

Renaming Fractions, Decimals, and Percents

REACHING MY GOAL
Rename percents and decimals as fractions, and rename fractions as percents or decimals. (MA.A.1.2.4)

How did I do?

A. You can write a percent or a decimal as a fraction or a mixed number.

Example 1

Write 2.125 as a fraction in simplest form.

Write the decimal as a mixed number.

$$2.125 = 2\frac{125}{1000}$$

Simplify the fraction.

$$= 2\frac{125 \div 125}{1000 \div 125}$$

$$= 2\frac{1}{\boxed{}}$$

Example 2

Rename 84% as a fraction in simplest form.

Write the percent as a fraction.

$$84\% = \frac{84}{\boxed{}}$$

Simplify.

$$= \frac{21}{\boxed{}}$$

B. You can write many fractions as percents. You can also write many fractions as decimals to the tenths, hundredths, or thousandths place.

Example 3

What percent is equivalent to $\frac{13}{20}$?

Rename the fraction as a fraction with a denominator of 100.

$$\frac{13}{20} \rightarrow \frac{13 \times 5}{20 \times 5} = \frac{\boxed{}}{100}$$

So, $\boxed{}$ % is equivalent to $\frac{13}{20}$.

> **THINK**
> If the denominator of a fraction is a factor of 100, you can easily rename it as a percent.

Example 4

What decimal is equivalent to $\frac{5}{8}$?

$\frac{5}{8} = \frac{?}{10}$ 8 does not divide 10.

$\frac{5}{8} = \frac{?}{100}$ 8 does not divide 100.

$\frac{5}{8} = \frac{?}{1000}$ 8 does divide 1,000. $\rightarrow$ $\frac{5 \times 125}{8 \times 125} = \frac{\boxed{}}{1000}$

So, 0.$\boxed{}$ is equivalent to $\frac{5}{8}$.

Practice

Rename the fraction as a percent.

1. $\dfrac{1}{4} \rightarrow \dfrac{1 \times \boxed{}}{4 \times \boxed{}} = \dfrac{\boxed{}}{100} \rightarrow \boxed{}\%$

2. $\dfrac{7}{10}$ ▢

3. $\dfrac{1}{2}$ ▢

4. $\dfrac{4}{5}$ ▢

5. $\dfrac{23}{25}$ ▢

6. $\dfrac{3}{4}$ ▢

Rename the fraction as a decimal.

7. $\dfrac{2}{5}$ 5 divides 10. $\rightarrow \dfrac{2 \times \boxed{}}{5 \times \boxed{}} = \dfrac{\boxed{}}{10} \rightarrow 0.\boxed{}$

8. $\dfrac{17}{20}$ ▢

9. $\dfrac{7}{8}$ ▢

10. $\dfrac{12}{25}$ ▢

11. $\dfrac{3}{40}$ ▢

12. $\dfrac{1}{2}$ ▢

Write the decimal or percent as a fraction in simplest form.

13. 90% ▢

14. 0.464 ▢

15. 20% ▢

16. 0.375 ▢

17. 72% ▢

Circle the letter of the three equivalent terms.

18. **F** 0.25, $\dfrac{2}{5}$, 40%

   G 0.06, $\dfrac{3}{5}$, 60%

   H 0.3, $\dfrac{3}{5}$, 30%

   I 0.6, $\dfrac{3}{5}$, 60%

19. **A** 35%, $\dfrac{1}{4}$, 0.35

   B 25%, $\dfrac{2}{8}$, 0.25

   C 25%, $\dfrac{1}{4}$, 0.2

   D 35%, $\dfrac{3}{8}$, 0.38

20. **F** $\dfrac{7}{100}$, 70%, 0.7

   G $\dfrac{7}{10}$, 7%, 0.7

   H $\dfrac{7}{10}$, 70%, 0.07

   I $\dfrac{7}{10}$, 70%, 0.7

21. **A** 0.05, $\dfrac{1}{20}$, 5%

   B 0.05, $\dfrac{1}{2}$, 50%

   C 0.5, $\dfrac{1}{20}$, 8%

   D 0.08, $\dfrac{1}{8}$, 8%

Problem Solving

A team of paleontologists spent the summer digging for fossils. **Use their bar graph to complete the circle graph: label each sector and write the percent. Answer the questions.**

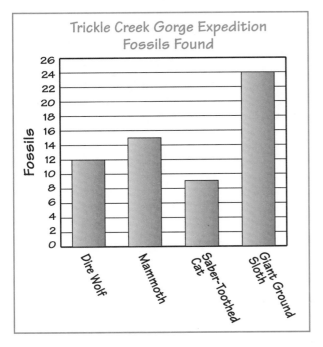

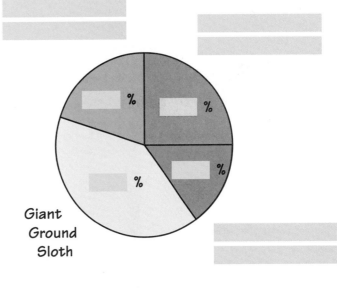

1. What percent of the fossils were from giant ground sloths?

   a. Find the fraction of the fossils that were from giant ground sloths.

   $\dfrac{24}{}$ ← Fossils of giant ground sloths
   ← All fossils

   b. Simplify the fraction, and rename it as a percent.
      _____ % of the fossils were from giant ground sloths.

2. Which kind of fossil made up the smallest percent of the fossils found?

3. Which two kinds of fossil together made up 40% of the total?

4. Which kind of fossil made up double the percent of the dire-wolf fossils?

5. Which animal accounted for twice as many fossils as the dire wolf?

   Suppose the paleontologists made another trip to Trickle Creek Gorge and found *double* the number of each kind of fossil. How would their new graphs differ from the ones on this page?

Connections

1. Write all of the whole-number factors of 100.

2. Write all of the whole-number factors of 1,000.

3. Draw enough 0.01-gram masses to balance the scale.

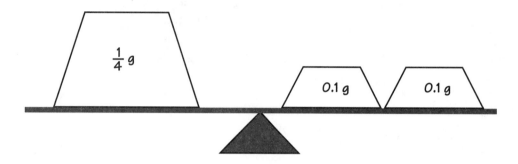

4. Draw enough $\frac{1}{4}$-ounce masses to balance the scale.

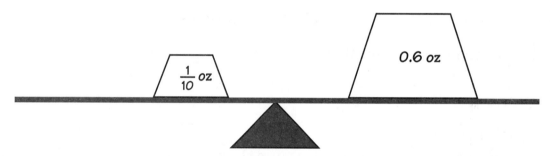

Find a fraction or decimal to complete the equation.

5. $\frac{3}{4} = 0.7 + \square$

6. $0.9 = \frac{1}{2} + \square$

7. $0.25 = \frac{1}{8} + \square$

8. $\frac{1}{2} = 0.3 + \square$

9. $\frac{7}{8} = 0.8 + \square$

10. $0.4 = \frac{2}{5} + \square$

Complete the sentences by writing 1, 2, 3, or 4. Use each number once.

11. ____ is divisible by ____ .

12. ____ divides ____ .

Approximating Fractions

REACHING MY GOAL
Compare and order fractions, decimals, and percents. (MA.A.1.2.2)

How did I do?

A. You can approximate a fraction, decimal, or percent by comparing it to the benchmarks $\frac{1}{4}$, $\frac{1}{2}$, and $\frac{3}{4}$.

Example 1

Use the table to approximate 0.31, $\frac{4}{7}$, and 82% as fractions.

$\frac{1}{4}$	25%	0.25

$\frac{1}{2}$	50%	0.5

$\frac{3}{4}$	75%	0.75

- 0.31 is close to 0.25, so it is approximately $\frac{}{}$.

- The numerator of $\frac{4}{7}$ is about half the denominator, so it is approximately $\frac{}{}$.

- 83% is close to 75%, so it is about $\frac{}{}$.

B. Approximating numbers can help you compare them. Keep track of whether each number is less than or more than the closest benchmark.

Example 2

Order $\frac{9}{16}$, 47%, and 0.8 from least to greatest.

- $\frac{9}{16}$ is close to $\frac{}{}$.

  9 is a little more than half of 16, so $\frac{9}{16}$ is a little *more than* $\frac{}{}$.

- 47% is a little less than 50%, so it is a little _____ than $\frac{1}{2}$.

- 0.8 is close to 0.75. It is a little more than 0.75, so it is a little _____ than $\frac{}{}$.

Write the three numbers on the number line.

So, from least to greatest, the numbers are _____ , _____ , and _____ .

Practice

1. Place each number in the box with the closest benchmark.

9%   0.68   30%   0.9 $\frac{23}{25}$ $\frac{9}{20}$ 0.22 $\frac{1}{16}$ 55% $\frac{7}{10}$

about 0   about $\frac{1}{4}$ about $\frac{1}{2}$ about $\frac{3}{4}$ about 1

2. Place each number on the number line. $\frac{27}{50}$ 0.28   5% $\frac{15}{16}$

0        $\frac{1}{4}$ $\frac{1}{2}$ $\frac{3}{4}$ 1

Mark the approximate location of each number on the number line. Then label the numbers.

3. 81%   0.46 $\frac{3}{32}$ 0.69

```
←———+————————+————————+————————+————————+———→
    0        1/4      1/2      3/4       1
```

4. $\frac{13}{24}$ 0.11 $\frac{9}{10}$ 19%

```
←———+————————+————————+————————+————————+———→
    0        1/4      1/2      3/4       1
```

Order the numbers from least to greatest.

5. 52%, $\frac{11}{26}$, $\frac{11}{12}$    6. $\frac{19}{20}$, $\frac{17}{30}$, 0.45

Problem Solving

Mr. Midlin, a math teacher, has an unusual way of grading his students. He gives five tests. He doesn't count the two highest scores of each student. Nor does he count the two lowest scores. He uses the middle score of each student to determine the student's grade. **Use the grading scale and the test scores to answer the questions.**

Mr. Midlin's Grading Scale

A 90% to 100%
B 80% to 89%
C 70% to 79%
D 60% to 69%

Students' Test Scores

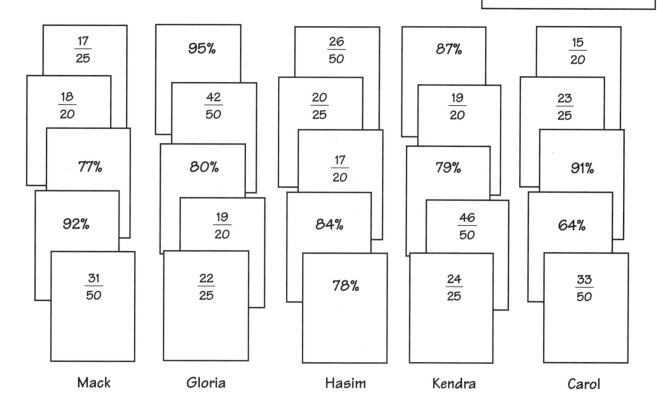

Mack Gloria Hasim Kendra Carol

1. What was Mack's grade for the class?

2. What was Gloria's grade for the class?

3. What was Hasim's grade for the class

4. What was Kendra's grade for the class?

5. What was Carol's grade for the class?

6. What grade would Mack have received if his 92% test score had been 97%?

7. What grade would Carol have received if her $\frac{33}{50}$ test score had been $\frac{43}{50}$?

8. To improve her grade by one letter, what is the lowest score Gloria would have needed on the test for which she scored $\frac{22}{25}$?

Connections

Use the advertisements to answer questions 1–4.

World of Beads	
Wood beads	$5/10
Tin beads	$8/15
Glass beads	$3/4
Ceramic beads	$2/9

Bead Universe	
Glass beads	$4 for 6
Ceramic beads	$4 for 12
Tin beads	$6 for 10
Wood beads	$3 for 20

1. Which store has the less expensive wood beads?

2. Which store has the less expensive glass beads?

3. Which store has the less expensive tin beads?

4. Which store has the less expensive ceramic beads?

ALGEBRA READINESS

Solve for x.

5. $\frac{1}{4} = x + 0.05$

$x =$

6. $0.3 + x = \frac{2}{5}$

$x =$

7. $x + 0.8 = \frac{7}{8}$

$x =$

8. $x + 0.1 = \frac{1}{2}$

$x =$

9. $\frac{9}{10} = x + 0.85$

$x =$

10. $0.6 + x = \frac{3}{4}$

$x =$

Draw masses of 0.1 kg and 0.05 kg to balance each balance. ⟋ 0.1 kg ⟍ ⟋ 0.05 kg ⟍

11.

12.

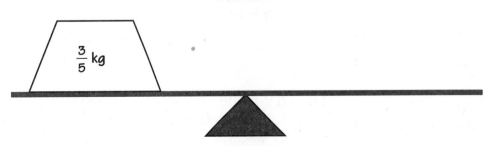

• TOPIC 6: Fractions, Mixed Numbers, and Percent Lesson 11

Comparing Fractions, Decimals, and Percents

REACHING MY GOAL
Compare and order fractions, decimals, and percents. (MA.A.1.2.2)

How did I do?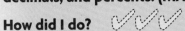

A. To compare numbers that are in different forms, first write them in the same form. Rename percents and fractions as decimals.

Example 1

Write $\frac{3}{5}$, 0.69, and 55% in order from least to greatest.

Step 1: Write the fraction as a decimal.

Think: 5 divides 10. I can write $\frac{3}{5}$ as a decimal to the tenths place.

$$\frac{3}{5} = \frac{?}{10} \rightarrow \frac{3 \times 2}{5 \times 2} = \frac{}{10} \rightarrow 0.6$$

Step 2: Write the percent as a decimal.

$$55\% \rightarrow \frac{}{100} = 0.55$$

Step 3: Compare. Write < or >.

0.55 ⬭ 0.6

0.6 ⬭ 0.69

So, from least to greatest, the numbers are 55%, _____, and _____.

B. If numbers are not very close in value, you can compare them without renaming. Mentally compare each number to the closest benchmark.

Example 2

Complete the benchmark table. Write 0.24, 82%, and $\frac{11}{20}$ in order from least to greatest. Show them on the number line.

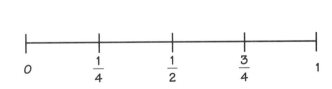

	25%	0.25
$\frac{1}{2}$		0.5
$\frac{3}{4}$	75%	

0.24 is a little less than 0.25.

82% is a little more than _____%.

$\frac{11}{20}$ is a little _____ than $\frac{1}{2}$.

So, from least to greatest, the numbers are 0.24, _____, and _____.

Practice

1. Compare $\frac{21}{24}$ and 80%.

   a. Simplify $\frac{21}{24}$, and rename it as a decimal.

   $$\frac{21 \div 3}{24 \div 3} = \frac{\boxed{}}{8}$$

   8 does not divide 10 or 100.

   8 does divide 1,000. $\frac{7 \times 125}{8 \times 125} \rightarrow \frac{\boxed{}}{1000} = 0.\boxed{}$

   b. Rename 80% as a decimal.

   $80\% \rightarrow \dfrac{\boxed{}}{100} = \boxed{}$

   c. Compare. $0.875 > 0.8$, so $\frac{21}{24}$ ⬭ 80%.

Compare. Write <, >, or =.

2. $\frac{3}{12}$ ⬭ 0.3

3. 2% ⬭ 0.1

4. $\frac{9}{10}$ ⬭ 90%

5. 0.29 ⬭ $\frac{18}{75}$

6. 64% ⬭ $\frac{2}{5}$

7. $\frac{3}{8}$ ⬭ 0.4

8. $\frac{17}{20}$ ⬭ 0.8

9. 75% ⬭ $\frac{12}{16}$

Write the numbers in order from least to greatest.

10. $\frac{3}{10}$, 52%, 0.22

11. 18%, 0.4, $\frac{6}{30}$

12. 0.89, $\frac{20}{32}$, 60%

13. $\frac{7}{20}$, 0.31, 33%

Solve.

14. Three friends caught night crawlers. Sam filled 0.79 of his container, Ann filled $\frac{3}{4}$ of her container, and Beth filled 80% of her container. Whose container was the least full?

15. On Monday, Rachel ran 66% of the distance to school. On Tuesday, she ran $\frac{3}{5}$ of the distance. On Wednesday, she ran 0.5 of the distance. On which day did Rachel run the farthest?

16. A scientist measured the mass of three rocks. A red rock had a mass of $\frac{1}{4}$ kg. A brown rock had a mass of 0.45 kg. A yellow rock had a mass equal to 9% of a kilogram. Which rock had the least mass?

17. In a basketball free-throw contest, each player got the same number of shots. Gustavo made 56% of his shots. Alan made $\frac{10}{16}$ of his shots. Charlie made 0.6 of his shots. Who made the most shots?

• TOPIC 6: Fractions, Mixed Numbers, and Percent Lesson 12

Problem Solving

Circle the letter of the correct answer.

1. Sal has 6 coins in his pocket. If they total 24% of a dollar, what fraction of the coins are dimes?

   A $\frac{1}{4}$ C $\frac{1}{2}$

   B $\frac{1}{3}$ D $\frac{2}{3}$

2. Cindy spent $\frac{9}{25}$ of a dollar on candy. What is the fewest number of coins she could have used?

   F 2   H 4

   G 3   I 5

3. At a store, Frank received 6 coins in change, totaling $0.54. What percent of a dollar were the pennies?

   A 4%   C 40%

   B 14%   D 44%

4. A bus ride costs $\frac{3}{5}$ of a dollar. How much does the ride cost?

   F $0.30   H $0.50

   G $0.40   I $0.60

5. Nilifur found 10 coins under her bed, totaling $0.71. Fifty percent of the coins were dimes. What percent of the coins were nickels?

   A 4%   C 40%

   B 20%   D 48%

6. Steve paid an overdue-book fine at the library with dimes and nickels. If the ratio of dimes to nickels was $\frac{4}{3}$, how much was the fine?

   F $0.50   H $0.60

   G $0.55   I $0.70

7. A magician took 15 coins out of his ear. The coins totaled $0.35. What fraction of the coins were pennies?

   A $\frac{3}{20}$ C $\frac{1}{3}$

   B $\frac{7}{20}$ D $\frac{2}{3}$

8. Yolanda has $0.50 in quarters and $0.50 in dimes. What is the ratio of quarters to dimes?

   F $\frac{1}{1}$ H $\frac{5}{2}$

   G $\frac{1}{5}$ I $\frac{2}{5}$

Morris's grandmother handed him a fifty-cent piece and said, "Here are four bits. Please buy me a plum." What fraction of a dollar is 1 bit?

Connections

Vera can win $1 million on a quiz program. **Read the information about her results so far, and complete the table. Then answer question 6.**

- She got 14 Cartoon Heroes questions right, and only 6 wrong.

- She got 6 of the 25 Rocks and Minerals questions wrong.

- The ratio of wrong to right answers for Australia was 3 to 7.

- She got $\frac{2}{10}$ of the Famous Farmers questions wrong.

- Of the 20 Cats and Ducks questions, she got 10 more right than she got wrong.

	VERA'S RESULTS		
	Category	Fraction Right	Percent Right
1.	Rocks and Minerals		
2.	Famous Farmers		
3.	Cartoon Heroes		
4.	Cats and Ducks		
5.	Australia		

6. Vera can choose any one of the categories for her last question. Which category should she pick?

ALGEBRA READINESS

Label each point on the number line.

7. 0.35, 70%, $\frac{7}{35}$, 5%, $\frac{9}{16}$

8. 0.6, $\frac{3}{4}$, 29%, $\frac{18}{20}$, 0.09

Adding and Subtracting Fractions

REACHING MY GOAL
Solve problems involving adding and subtracting fractions. (MA.A.3.2.3)

How did I do?

A. You can add or subtract fractions by adding or subtracting the parts, as long as the fractions have the same denominator.

Example 1

Mae has a rectangular garden. She has planted $\frac{3}{8}$ of the garden with tulips. She has enough tulip bulbs to plant $\frac{4}{8}$ more of the garden. **If she plants all the remaining bulbs, how much of the garden will Mae have planted in all?**

Shade 3 eighths to show the tulips already planted.

Shade 4 more eighths of the garden.

Now you can count or add the numerators to find the total.

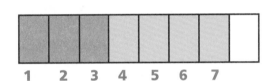

$$\frac{3}{8} + \frac{4}{8} = \frac{7}{8}$$

Mae will have planted ▨ of the garden in all.

B. When you find a sum or a difference, you may want to write it in simplest form. This will help if you need to do more adding or subtracting or use the answer in a comparison.

Example 2

Is $\frac{7}{8} - \frac{3}{8}$ less than $\frac{2}{3}$?

$\frac{7}{8} - \frac{3}{8} = \frac{4}{8}$, or $\frac{1}{2}$ $\frac{1}{2} < \frac{2}{3}$ So, $\frac{7}{8} - \frac{3}{8} < \frac{2}{3}$.

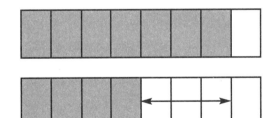

C. If a sum is greater than 1, it should be written as a mixed number.

Example 3

Find the sum of $\frac{3}{4}$ and $\frac{2}{4}$.

$\frac{3}{4} + \frac{2}{4} = \frac{5}{4}$, or $1\frac{1}{4}$

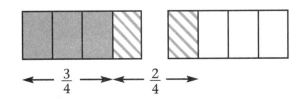

Practice

Add or subtract.

1. $\frac{3}{5} + \frac{1}{5} = \frac{?}{5}$

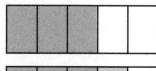

$\frac{3}{5} + \frac{1}{5} = \frac{\blacksquare}{5}$

2. $\frac{3}{4} - \frac{1}{2} = \frac{?}{4}$

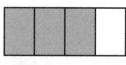

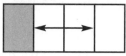

$\frac{3}{4} - \frac{1}{2} = \frac{\blacksquare}{4}$

Shade the diagram. Then add or subtract.

3. $\frac{1}{6} + \frac{4}{6} = \frac{?}{6}$

$\frac{1}{6} + \frac{4}{6} = \frac{\blacksquare}{6}$

4. $\frac{2}{3} + \frac{2}{3} = \frac{?}{3}$

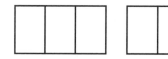

$\frac{2}{3} + \frac{2}{3} = \frac{\blacksquare}{3}$, or $1\frac{\blacksquare}{3}$

5. $\frac{5}{6} - \frac{2}{6} = \frac{?}{6}$

$\frac{5}{6} - \frac{2}{6} = \frac{\blacksquare}{6}$, or $\frac{\blacksquare}{2}$

6. $\frac{7}{8} - \frac{2}{8} = \frac{?}{8}$

$\frac{7}{8} - \frac{2}{8} = \frac{\blacksquare}{8}$

Solve.

7. $\frac{3}{5} + \frac{3}{5} = \frac{\blacksquare}{5}$, or $1\frac{\blacksquare}{5}$

8. $\frac{4}{5} - \frac{2}{5} = \frac{\blacksquare}{5}$

9. $\frac{7}{8} - \frac{5}{8} = \frac{\blacksquare}{\blacksquare}$, or $\frac{\blacksquare}{\blacksquare}$

10. $\frac{2}{5} + \frac{4}{5} = \frac{\blacksquare}{\blacksquare}$, or $\blacksquare\frac{\blacksquare}{\blacksquare}$

11. $\frac{3}{4} - \frac{2}{4} = \frac{\blacksquare}{\blacksquare}$

12. $\frac{2}{6} + \frac{3}{6} = \frac{\blacksquare}{\blacksquare}$

13. $\frac{2}{4} + \frac{3}{4} = \frac{\blacksquare}{\blacksquare}$, or $\blacksquare\frac{\blacksquare}{\blacksquare}$

14. $\frac{4}{5} - \frac{1}{5} = \frac{\blacksquare}{\blacksquare}$

Problem Solving

Solve.

1. Farmer Lander uses $\frac{2}{5}$ of his land to raise ducks. This year, the farmer opened another $\frac{2}{5}$ of his land to raise geese. How much of the land is used to raise ducks and geese?

2. Jeb had planted $\frac{6}{8}$ of his garden with snap beans. During a thunderstorm, the snap-bean plants in $\frac{2}{8}$ of the garden were washed away. What fraction of the garden still had snap beans?

3. Jae served $\frac{2}{6}$ of a pizza. Then she served $\frac{3}{6}$ of the pizza. How much of the pizza was left?

4. Lila had $\frac{3}{4}$ of a ream of paper. Jill gave her another $\frac{3}{4}$ of a ream. How much paper did Lila have then?

5. Jeff had filled $\frac{1}{2}$ of an ice-cube tray when the phone rang. Jeff answered the call. How much of the tray did he still have to fill?

6. Pat used $\frac{4}{12}$ of a carton of eggs. Her brother Jim used $\frac{3}{12}$ of the carton of eggs. What fraction of the carton of eggs remained?

7. Del had $\frac{7}{16}$ lb of shrimp. Mel gave him some of her shrimp. Now Del has $\frac{15}{16}$ lb of shrimp. How many pounds of shrimp did Mel give to Del?

8. In Hill's aquarium, $\frac{1}{8}$ of the fish are red, $\frac{5}{8}$ of the fish are striped, and the rest of the fish are gold. What fraction of the fish are gold?

9. Gia walked $\frac{3}{10}$ of a mile by noon. At 6:00 P.M., she had walked $1\frac{1}{10}$ of a mile. What distance did she walk between noon and 6:00 P.M.?

10. Mia had packages that weighed $\frac{4}{16}$ lb and $\frac{5}{16}$ lb. Dan had packages that weighed $\frac{1}{4}$ lb and $\frac{3}{4}$ lb. Whose packages weighed more?

Connections

Compare. Write <, >, or =.

1. $\frac{230}{1000} + \frac{68}{1000}$ ⬭ $0.200 + 0.059$

2. $\frac{360}{1000} - \frac{340}{1000}$ ⬭ $0.350 - 0.310$

3. $\frac{35}{100} + \frac{30}{100}$ ⬭ $0.350 + 0.29$

4. $\frac{54}{100} - \frac{17}{100}$ ⬭ $0.66 - 0.29$

Use the circle graph to solve problems 5–8.

5. How much more money did Jan spend on a radio than she spent on CDs?

6. Jan first bought the shirt. The next purchase she made brought her spending to $40. What was her second purchase?

7. How much more did Jan spend on books and CDs than she spent on pens and a radio?

8. Was the amount that Jan spent on pens, CDs, and books less than, equal to, or greater than the amount she spent on a shirt and a radio?

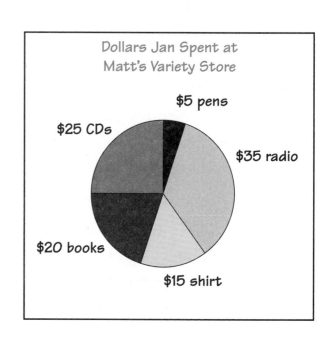

Dollars Jan Spent at Matt's Variety Store

$5 pens
$25 CDs
$35 radio
$20 books
$15 shirt

ALGEBRA READINESS

Write the missing addend.

9. $\frac{3}{10} + \underline{\hphantom{0}} = \frac{7}{10}$

10. $\underline{\hphantom{0}} + \frac{64}{100} = \frac{99}{100}$

11. $\frac{60}{100} + \underline{\hphantom{0}} = \frac{88}{100}$

12. $\underline{\hphantom{0}} + \frac{130}{1000} = \frac{550}{1000}$

13. $\frac{130}{1000} + \underline{\hphantom{0}} = \frac{670}{1000}$

14. $\underline{\hphantom{0}} + \frac{25}{100} = \frac{83}{100}$

Adding and Subtracting with Fractions, Mixed Numbers, and Whole Numbers

One way to add or subtract with fractions and mixed numbers is to count on or count back.

A. When you add a whole number to a number or subtract a whole number from a number, you can count on or back by whole units.

Example 1

Add $5\frac{1}{3} + 2$.

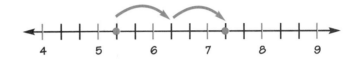

Step 1: Mark $5\frac{1}{3}$ on a number line.

Step 2: Count on by ones. $5\frac{1}{3} + 1 + 1 = 7\frac{1}{3}$

So, $5\frac{1}{3} + 2 = 7\frac{1}{3}$.

Example 2

Subtract $5\frac{1}{4} - 2$.

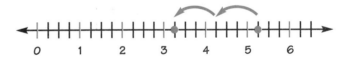

Step 1: Mark $5\frac{1}{4}$ on the number line.

Step 2: Count back by ones. $5\frac{1}{4} - 1 - 1 = 3\frac{1}{4}$

So, $5\frac{1}{4} - 2 = \boxed{}\frac{1}{4}$.

B. To subtract a fraction from a number, count back by the fractional unit.

Example 3

Subtract $2\frac{3}{4} - \frac{1}{4}$.

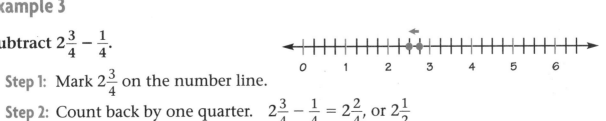

Step 1: Mark $2\frac{3}{4}$ on the number line.

Step 2: Count back by one quarter. $2\frac{3}{4} - \frac{1}{4} = 2\frac{2}{4}$, or $2\frac{1}{2}$

So, $2\frac{3}{4} - \frac{1}{4} = 2\boxed{}$.

Practice

Subtract.

1. $4 - \frac{2}{3}$

   a. Begin at the 4 on the number line.

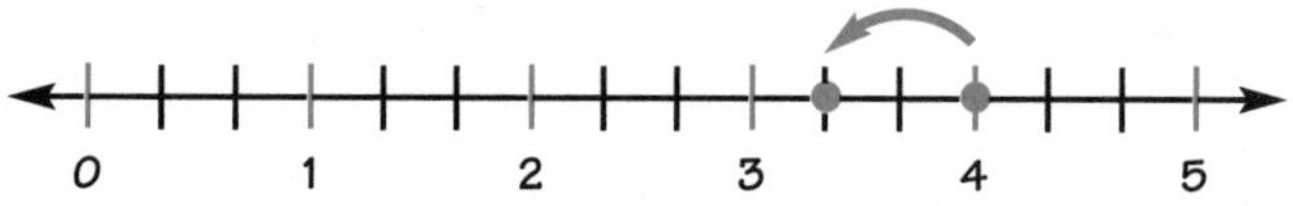

   b. Count back 2 thirds.

   So, $4 - \frac{2}{3} = 3$ ____

2. $2 - \frac{3}{4} =$ ____

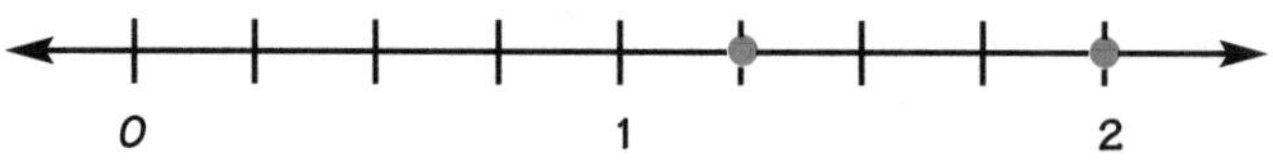

3. $1\frac{3}{4} - 1 =$ ____

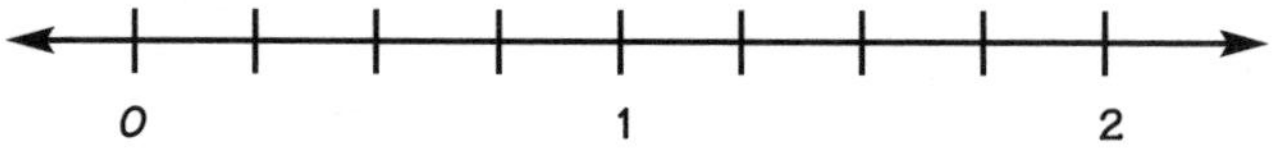

4. $8\frac{1}{3} - \frac{2}{3} =$ ____

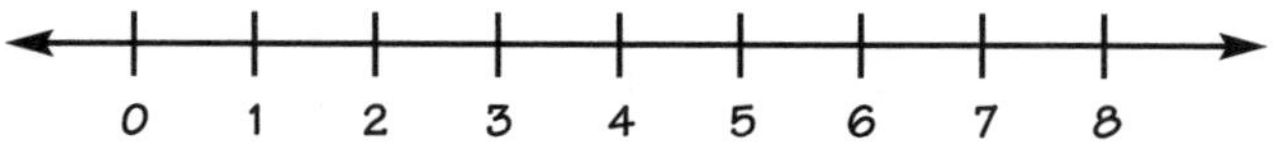

5. $5 - \frac{3}{4} =$ ____

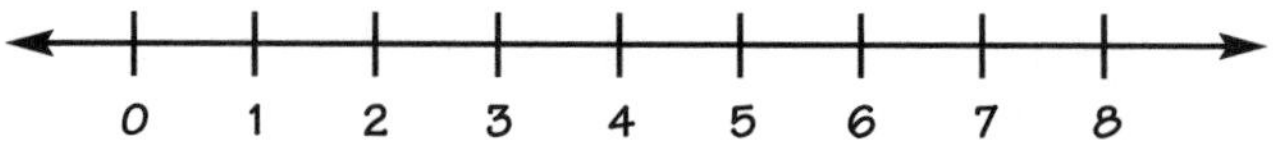

Find the sum or the difference.

6. $3\frac{3}{8} + 6 =$ ____
7. $5\frac{3}{5} - \frac{2}{5} =$ ____
8. $7\frac{9}{10} - \frac{7}{10} =$ ____
9. $8\frac{2}{3} + 3 =$ ____
10. $4\frac{5}{8} - 2 =$ ____
11. $4\frac{3}{7} + \frac{2}{7} =$ ____
12. $11\frac{4}{5} + 3 =$ ____
13. $8\frac{7}{8} - 3 =$ ____
14. $6\frac{2}{3} - \frac{1}{3} =$ ____
15. $9 + 3\frac{5}{6} =$ ____
16. $4\frac{3}{5} + \frac{1}{5} =$ ____
17. $5\frac{1}{4} - \frac{3}{4} =$ ____
18. $2\frac{5}{8} + 4 =$ ____
19. $6\frac{4}{5} - 5 =$ ____
20. $1\frac{3}{10} + 7 =$ ____

Problem Solving

The object of this game is to choose functions that change a starting number into a target number. Here are the three functions that you can use.

Function A: $x - 1$

Function B: $x - \dfrac{1}{4}$

Function C: $x - \dfrac{1}{3}$

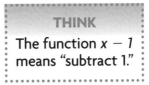

THINK

The function $x - 1$ means "subtract 1."

You can use any or all of the functions up to 4 times to change the starting number to the target number. The first run through the function machine is done for you.

Function Machine

	Starting Number	Turn 1	Turn 2	Turn 3	Turn 4	Target Number
1.	$7\dfrac{1}{4}$	Function A $7\dfrac{1}{4} - 1 = 6\dfrac{1}{4}$	Function B $6\dfrac{1}{4} - \dfrac{1}{4} = 6$			6
2.	$2\dfrac{1}{3}$					$1\dfrac{1}{3}$
3.	$5\dfrac{1}{2}$					$3\dfrac{1}{4}$
4.	$9\dfrac{1}{3}$					$8\dfrac{2}{3}$
5.	$12\dfrac{2}{3}$					10
6.	15					$13\dfrac{1}{4}$

Connections

Solve.

1. Jay had 15.8 oz of guava juice. He poured 13 oz of the juice into a pitcher. How many ounces of guava juice did Jay have left?

2. Mila had 11.6 yd of silk. She bought 2 yd more to make a dress. How many yards of material did she have?

3. Shayla cut 0.2 in. from an 8-in. board to make a shelf. What was the length of the finished shelf?

4. Del measured 4 oz of flour for a recipe. Then he measured 0.8 oz more. How much flour did he measure altogether?

5. A jetliner flew 3,000 mi to the west and then flew 250 mi to the east. How far from the starting point was the jetliner?

6. A ship sailed 3,850 mi to the south and then sailed 50 mi to the north. How far from the starting point was the ship?

ALGEBRA READINESS

Find the missing number.

7. $8\frac{3}{10} -$ ____ $= 5\frac{3}{10}$

8. $6 -$ ____ $= 5\frac{1}{3}$

9. $4\frac{1}{3} +$ ____ $= 5$

10. ____ $+ \frac{3}{8} = 6$

11. ____ $- 3 = 3\frac{2}{3}$

12. ____ $+ 4 = 7\frac{2}{3}$

13. $7\frac{3}{10} +$ ____ $= 10\frac{3}{10}$

14. $9\frac{5}{6} -$ ____ $= 9\frac{1}{6}$

15. ____ $+ \frac{1}{5} = 4\frac{4}{5}$

16. $4 -$ ____ $= 3\frac{1}{8}$

LANGUAGE OF MATHEMATICS

Complete.

17. The sum of 5 and $\frac{2}{3}$ is ____.

18. The difference of 2 and $\frac{1}{4}$ is ____.

19. $\frac{1}{5}$ more than 3 is ____.

20. $\frac{3}{4}$ less than 2 is ____.

Adding and Subtracting Mixed Numbers

REACHING MY GOAL
Solve problems involving adding and subtracting with mixed numbers and fractions. (MA.A.3.2.3)

How did I do? ✓✓✓

When you add or subtract mixed numbers, add or subtract the whole-number part first.

Example 1

Kim placed stones for $1\frac{2}{3}$ yards of a walkway and then placed another $1\frac{2}{3}$ yards of stones. **What was the length of the finished walkway?**

Step 1: Add the whole numbers first.

$$1\frac{2}{3} \quad + \quad 1\frac{2}{3}$$

$$\underbrace{1\frac{2}{3} \;+\; 1} \;+\; \underbrace{\frac{2}{3}}$$

$$2\frac{2}{3} \;+\; \frac{2}{3}$$

> **THINK**
> I need to find $1\frac{2}{3} + 1\frac{2}{3}$.

Step 2: Break $\frac{2}{3}$ so you can bridge to the number 3 and add the fractional part.

$$2\frac{2}{3} \quad + \quad \frac{2}{3}$$

$$\underbrace{2\frac{2}{3} \;+\; \frac{1}{3}} \;+\; \frac{1}{3}$$

$$3 \;+\; \frac{1}{3} \;=\; 3\frac{1}{3}$$

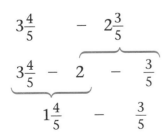

The length of the finished walkway was _____ yards.

Example 2

The road from Taylorville to Barkston is $3\frac{4}{5}$ miles long. Sal drove $2\frac{3}{5}$ miles and stopped. **How much farther did Sal have to drive to reach Barkston?**

Step 1: Subtract the whole number first.

$$3\frac{4}{5} \quad - \quad 2\frac{3}{5}$$

$$\underbrace{3\frac{4}{5} \;-\; 2} \;-\; \frac{3}{5}$$

$$1\frac{4}{5} \;-\; \frac{3}{5}$$

> **THINK**
> I need to find $3\frac{4}{5} - 2\frac{3}{5}$.

Step 2: Subtract the fractional part.

$$1\frac{4}{5} - \frac{3}{5} = 1\frac{1}{5}$$

Sal had to drive _____ miles farther to reach Barkston.

Practice

Find the sum or the difference. Use the number lines if you wish.

1. $4\frac{1}{4} - 2\frac{3}{4}$

Step 1: Subtract the whole number first.

$$4\frac{1}{4} \quad - \quad 2\frac{3}{4}$$

$$4\frac{1}{4} \; - \; 2 \; - \; \frac{3}{4}$$

$$2\frac{1}{4} \qquad - \quad \frac{3}{4}$$

Step 2: Break $\frac{3}{4}$ so you can bridge to 2.

$$2\frac{1}{4} \qquad - \qquad \frac{3}{4}$$

$$2\frac{1}{4} \; - \; \frac{1}{4} \; - \; \frac{2}{4}$$

$$2 \; - \; \frac{2}{4} \; = \; 1\frac{\boxed{}}{4}$$

$$1\frac{2}{4} \; = \; 1\frac{\boxed{}}{\boxed{}}$$

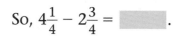

So, $4\frac{1}{4} - 2\frac{3}{4} = \boxed{}$.

2. $1\frac{1}{3} + 3\frac{1}{3} = 4\frac{\boxed{}}{\boxed{}}$

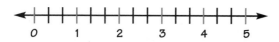

3. $4\frac{2}{5} - 1\frac{3}{5} = 2\frac{\boxed{}}{\boxed{}}$

4. $2\frac{3}{4} + 2\frac{3}{4} = 5\frac{\boxed{}}{\boxed{}}$, or $5\frac{\boxed{}}{\boxed{}}$

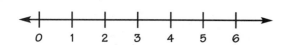

5. $3\frac{2}{5} - 2\frac{3}{5} = \frac{\boxed{}}{\boxed{}}$

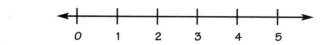

6. $1\frac{2}{3} + 2\frac{2}{3} = \boxed{}$

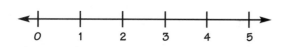

7. $4\frac{5}{6} - 2\frac{3}{6} = \boxed{}$, or $\boxed{}$

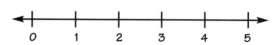

Find the sum or the difference.

8. $3\frac{1}{4} + 5\frac{3}{4} = \boxed{}$

9. $6\frac{4}{5} - 5\frac{1}{5} = \boxed{}$

10. $4\frac{5}{6} + 1\frac{2}{6} = \boxed{}$

11. $7\frac{5}{8} - 3\frac{7}{8} = \boxed{}$, or $\boxed{}$

Problem Solving

Solve.

1. Which two ingredients total 2 cups?

   _____

2. Which two ingredients total $\frac{3}{4}$ cup?

   _____

   Recipe for Trail Mix

$1\frac{1}{4}$ c rice cereal squares	$\frac{1}{4}$ c peanuts
$1\frac{3}{4}$ c corn cereal squares	$2\frac{3}{4}$ c almonds
$2\frac{1}{4}$ c dried berries	$\frac{1}{2}$ c raisins
$2\frac{1}{4}$ c pumpkin seeds	

3. How much more of the corn squares than the rice squares does the recipe call for?

   _____

4. Mai wants to make twice the amount of this recipe. How many cups of pumpkin seeds should she use?

   _____

5. Mai still plans to double the recipe. How many cups total of peanuts and raisins should Mai use?

   _____

6. Cal made the trail mix from the original recipe. How many more cups of almonds than of corn squares did he use?

   _____

7. Will the recipe produce less than 8 cups of trail mix, exactly 8 cups, or more than 8 cups of trail mix? How do you know?

   _____

8. How can you find the total number of cups of trail mix the recipe will make? What is the total number of cups?

   _____

9. How many more cups are there in the ingredient that is the greatest amount than in the ingredient that is the least?

   _____

10. Kim does not want to use corn squares. She wants to use extra almonds instead. How many cups of almonds will she use in all?

    _____

    If two mixed numbers have a difference that is a whole number, what can you tell about the numbers?

Connections

Solve.

1. Will had 3 reams of paper. He gave $\frac{3}{4}$ of a ream to Sue. How many reams did Will have left? ▨

2. Jen baked 5 pizzas. She served $\frac{3}{8}$ of a pizza. How many pizzas did she have left? ▨

Find the difference.

3. $7 - \frac{3}{5} =$ ▨

4. $4 - \frac{5}{6} =$ ▨

5. $10 - \frac{2}{3} =$ ▨

6. $3 - \frac{7}{8} =$ ▨

7. $2 - \frac{5}{8} =$ ▨

8. $13 - \frac{3}{4} =$ ▨

ALGEBRA READINESS

Solve.

9. $2\frac{3}{5} +$ ▨ $= 3$

10. $9\frac{6}{8} +$ ▨ $= 10$

11. $6\frac{1}{6} +$ ▨ $= 7$

12. $4\frac{2}{3} +$ ▨ $= 5$

Write the weight needed to balance the scale.

13. Weight needed: ▨

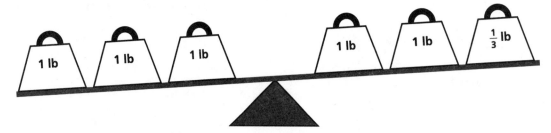

14. Weight needed: ▨

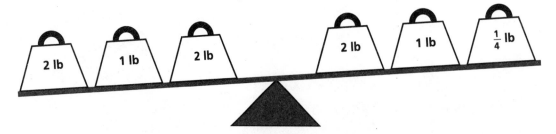

Estimating Sums and Differences of Fractions and Mixed Numbers

REACHING MY GOAL
Use benchmark numbers to estimate sums and differences of fractions and mixed numbers. (MA.A.4.2.1)

How did I do?

You can use the benchmarks 0, $\frac{1}{2}$, and 1 to estimate sums and differences of fractions and mixed numbers.

Example 1

Estimate the sum of $\frac{5}{8}$ and $\frac{5}{6}$.

$\frac{5}{8}$ is a little more than $\frac{1}{2}$. $\frac{5}{6}$ is a little less than 1.

So, the sum is about $\frac{1}{2} + 1$, or 1 ▢.

Example 2

Estimate the difference of $3\frac{7}{8}$ and $2\frac{1}{2}$.

Think: $3\frac{7}{8}$ is about 4. So, $4 - 2\frac{1}{2}$ is a good estimate.

Subtract the whole number first.

$4 - 2\frac{1}{2} \rightarrow 4 - 2 - \frac{1}{2} \rightarrow 2 - \boxed{}$, or $1\frac{1}{2}$

You can use a number line to visualize the estimate.

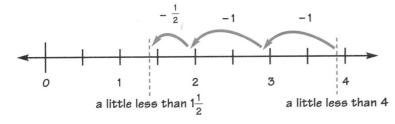

a little less than $1\frac{1}{2}$ a little less than 4

> **THINK**
> $3\frac{7}{8}$ is a little *less* than 4, so the difference will be a little *less* than $1\frac{1}{2}$.

Example 3

Estimate the sum of $1\frac{1}{8}$ and $2\frac{1}{3}$.

$1\frac{1}{8}$ is a little more than 1. $2\frac{1}{3}$ is a little less than $2\frac{1}{2}$.

So, the sum is about $1 + 2\frac{1}{2}$, or ▢ .

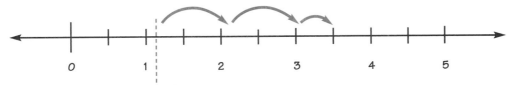

Example 4

Estimate $2\frac{3}{4} + 5\frac{1}{4} + 1\frac{1}{2} + 2\frac{1}{3}$.

Separate the whole and fractional parts of the mixed numbers.

$2 + 5 + 1 + 2 \qquad + \qquad \frac{3}{4} + \frac{1}{4} \qquad + \qquad \frac{1}{2} + \frac{1}{3}$

$\underbrace{}_{10} \qquad + \qquad \underbrace{\phantom{\frac{3}{4} + \frac{1}{4}}}_{1} \qquad + \qquad \underbrace{\text{about } 1} \qquad \rightarrow \qquad \text{about } \boxed{}$

Practice

Estimate the sum or the difference. Write *less than* $\frac{1}{2}$, *between* $\frac{1}{2}$ *and 1*, *between 1 and* $1\frac{1}{2}$, or *between* $1\frac{1}{2}$ *and 2* for the sum or the difference.

1. $\frac{3}{5} + \frac{5}{8}$

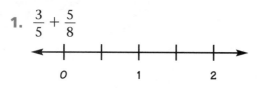

2. $\frac{7}{8} - \frac{2}{3}$

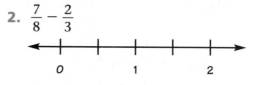

3. $\frac{3}{4} - \frac{1}{8}$

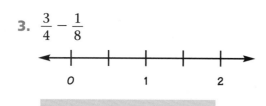

4. $\frac{7}{8} + \frac{5}{6}$

Estimate the sum or the difference. Circle the letter of the correct answer.

5. $2\frac{3}{5} + 4\frac{7}{8}$

    A about 5   **C** about 8

    B about $7\frac{1}{2}$ **D** about $8\frac{1}{2}$

6. $4\frac{5}{8} - 3\frac{1}{2}$

    F about 1   **H** about 3

    G about 2   **I** about 4

7. $9\frac{3}{5} + 4\frac{1}{4}$

    A about 13   **C** about 14

    B about $13\frac{1}{2}$ **D** about $14\frac{1}{2}$

8. $12\frac{2}{3} - 7\frac{1}{7}$

    F about 5   **H** about 6

    G about $5\frac{1}{2}$ **I** about $6\frac{1}{2}$

Estimate the sum.

9. $1\frac{2}{3} + 2\frac{1}{2} + 3\frac{4}{5}$

10. $1\frac{3}{5} + 6\frac{3}{4} + 8\frac{1}{8}$

11. $7\frac{3}{5} + 6\frac{1}{5} + 4\frac{1}{10}$

12. $2\frac{1}{3} + 2\frac{1}{4} + 2\frac{5}{6}$

Problem Solving

Use the map to estimate the distances.

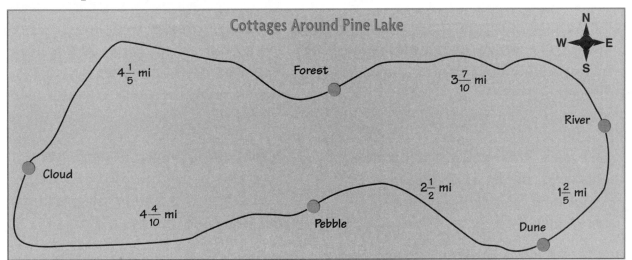

Cottages Around Pine Lake

$4\frac{1}{5}$ mi — Forest — $3\frac{7}{10}$ mi — River

Cloud

$4\frac{4}{10}$ mi — Pebble — $2\frac{1}{2}$ mi — Dune — $1\frac{2}{5}$ mi

1. Bill hiked east from Pebble. He stopped at River. About how far did he hike?

2. Dana hiked east from Dune, all the way to Cloud. About how far did she hike?

3. Sal hiked west from Pebble. About how far did he hike if he stopped at Forest?

4. About how long is the shorter hike between Cloud and Dune?

5. Which is the shorter hike from Forest to Pebble: through Cloud or through River?

6. Which cottage is closer to River: Forest or Pebble?

Circle the letter of the correct answer.

7. About how much farther is it from Forest to Dune than it is from Pebble to Dune?

   A about 2 mi

   B about $2\frac{1}{2}$ mi

   C about 3 mi

   D about $3\frac{1}{2}$ mi

8. About how many miles would you hike if you went the whole way around Pine Lake?

   F less than 15 mi

   G between 15 mi and 16 mi

   H between 16 mi and 17 mi

   I between 17 mi and 18 mi

Connections

Estimate the sum or the difference.

1. On Monday, Cary ran 3.2 k. On Tuesday, he ran 7.9 k, and on Friday, he ran 2.5 k. About how far did he run altogether?

2. Austin is 4.3 miles from Porter. Sayers is 12.9 miles from Porter. About how much farther from Porter is Sayers than Austin?

3. Last week, Phil ran 23.25 kilometers. This week, he ran 31.95 kilometers. About how many kilometers did he run in all?

4. Mara used 27.09 mg of magnesium in an experiment. Ann used 31.98 mg. About how much more magnesium did Ann use?

5. $5.7 + 9.1 + 8.9$

6. $34.8 - 25.2$

7. $2.8 + 8.2 + 11.1$

8. $12.7 - 2.9$

Write the letter of the figure that has the greatest perimeter. Use estimation.

9.

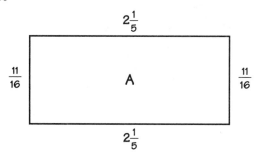
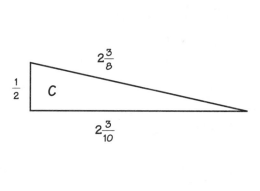

Figure _____ has the greatest perimeter.

ALGEBRA READINESS

Write <, >, or =.

10. $3\frac{1}{8} + \frac{2}{3}$ $3\frac{1}{4} + \frac{2}{3}$

11. $2\frac{1}{4} + 4\frac{1}{3}$ $4\frac{3}{4} + 2\frac{7}{8}$

12. $7\frac{1}{4} - 2\frac{1}{8}$ ⬭ $7\frac{1}{4} - 2\frac{2}{3}$

13. $4\frac{5}{6} - 3\frac{2}{5}$ ⬭ $5\frac{3}{8} - 4\frac{3}{4}$

• TOPIC 6: Fractions, Mixed Numbers, and Percent Lesson 16

Adding and Subtracting Unlike Fractions

REACHING MY GOAL
Add and subtract fractions that have unlike denominators. (MA.A.3.2.3)

How did I do?

Fractions that have different denominators are called unlike fractions. When you add or subtract unlike fractions, you first need to rename one or both fractions so that the fractions have the same denominator.

Example 1

$\frac{1}{2} + \frac{2}{3} = \square$

Step 1: Rename both fractions so that they have the same denominator.

Think: You can multiply the two denominators to find a common denominator.

$$\frac{1}{2} \rightarrow \frac{1 \times 3}{2 \times 3} \rightarrow \frac{3}{6}$$

$$\frac{2}{3} \rightarrow \frac{2 \times \square}{3 \times \square} \rightarrow \frac{4}{6}$$

Step 2: Separate the second addend into parts that make addition easy.

Think: $\frac{3}{6} + \frac{4}{6} > 1$. So, I'll break $\frac{4}{6}$ into parts to bridge to 1.

$\frac{3}{6} + \square = 1$? You need to add $\frac{3}{6}$.

So, break $\frac{4}{6}$ into $\frac{3}{6} + \frac{1}{6}$.

$$\frac{3}{6} + \frac{4}{6} \rightarrow \frac{3}{6} + \frac{3}{6} + \frac{1}{6}$$

Step 3: Add.

$$\frac{3}{6} + \frac{3}{6} + \frac{1}{6} \rightarrow 1 + \frac{1}{6} = 1\frac{1}{6}$$

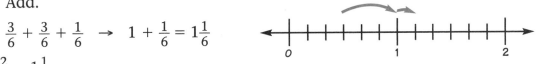

So, $\frac{1}{2} + \frac{2}{3} = 1\frac{1}{6}$.

Example 2

$\frac{4}{5} - \frac{1}{3} = \square$

Step 1: Rename both fractions so that they have the same denominator.

$$\frac{4}{5} \rightarrow \frac{4 \times 3}{5 \times 3} \rightarrow \frac{12}{15}$$

$$\frac{1}{3} \rightarrow \frac{1 \times \square}{3 \times \square} \rightarrow \frac{5}{15}$$

Step 2: Subtract.

$$\frac{12}{15} - \frac{5}{15} = \frac{7}{15}$$

So, $\frac{4}{5} - \frac{1}{3} = \underline{}$.

Practice

Find the sum or the difference.

1. $\frac{1}{3} + \frac{1}{6}$

   a. Rename both fractions so that they have the same denominator.

   $$\frac{1}{3} + \frac{1}{6} \quad \rightarrow \quad \frac{2}{6} + \frac{1}{6}$$

   b. Add.

   $$\frac{2}{6} + \frac{1}{6} = \frac{3}{6}, \text{ or } \frac{1}{2}$$

   So, $\frac{1}{3} + \frac{1}{6} = \frac{1}{\boxed{}}$.

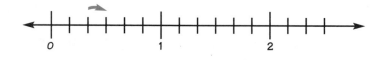

2. $\frac{1}{2} - \frac{1}{5}$

   a. Rename both fractions so that they have the same denominator.

   $$\frac{1}{2} - \frac{1}{5} \quad \rightarrow \quad \frac{5}{10} - \frac{2}{10}$$

   b. Subtract.

   $$\frac{5}{10} - \frac{2}{10} = \frac{\boxed{}}{10}$$

   So, $\frac{1}{2} - \frac{1}{5} = \boxed{}$.

3. $\frac{1}{4} + \frac{2}{8} = $

4. $\frac{3}{5} - \frac{1}{4} = $

5. $\frac{3}{4} + \frac{2}{3} = $

6. $\frac{1}{2} - \frac{1}{5} = $

7. $\frac{1}{3} + \frac{2}{5} = $

8. $\frac{3}{4} - \frac{1}{8} = $

9. $\frac{2}{5} + \frac{2}{6} = $

10. $\frac{5}{9} - \frac{1}{3} = $

11. $\frac{5}{8} + \frac{5}{6} = $

12. $\frac{5}{6} - \frac{5}{8} = $

How would you separate $\frac{10}{12} + \frac{9}{12} + \frac{6}{12}$ to make the addition easy?

Problem Solving

Use the recipe to solve the problems.

Multigrain Miniloaf	
$\frac{1}{4}$ oz dry yeast	$\frac{1}{2}$ c wheat flour
$\frac{1}{8}$ oz honey	$\frac{1}{3}$ c soy flour
$\frac{3}{4}$ c water	$\frac{1}{8}$ c poppy seeds
$\frac{1}{8}$ c white flour	$\frac{1}{4}$ c sesame seeds
$\frac{1}{4}$ c rye flour	$\frac{3}{8}$ c flax seeds

1. How many cups of seeds are called for by the recipe?

2. How many cups of flour does the recipe call for?

3. How many more cups of flour than cups of seeds does the recipe call for?

4. If the recipe were doubled, how much soy flour would be needed?

5. If the recipe were tripled, what amount of sesame seeds would be needed?

6. If the recipe were tripled, what amount of wheat flour would be needed?

7. How much more wheat flour than rye flour does the recipe call for?

8. How much more wheat flour than soy flour does the recipe call for?

9. If the recipe were doubled, what amount of flax seeds would be needed?

10. If the recipe were doubled, what total amount of seeds would be needed?

11. If the recipe were doubled, what amount of water would be needed?

12. If the recipe were doubled, how much yeast and honey would be needed?

Connections

Find the sum.

1. $\dfrac{3}{100} + \dfrac{7}{10} + \dfrac{9}{1000}$

2. $\dfrac{4}{10} + \dfrac{3}{1000} + \dfrac{5}{100}$

3. $\dfrac{7}{1000} + \dfrac{3}{10} + \dfrac{6}{100}$

4. $\dfrac{2}{100} + \dfrac{9}{1000} + \dfrac{9}{10}$

5. $\dfrac{1}{2} + \dfrac{1}{4} + \dfrac{3}{8}$

6. $\dfrac{1}{2} + \dfrac{1}{3} + \dfrac{1}{6}$

7. $\dfrac{1}{2} + \dfrac{1}{5} + \dfrac{1}{10}$

8. $\dfrac{1}{2} + \dfrac{1}{4} + \dfrac{1}{8}$

ALGEBRA READINESS

Write <, >, or =.

9. $\dfrac{1}{2} + \left(\dfrac{1}{3} + \dfrac{1}{4}\right)$ ⬭ $\left(\dfrac{1}{2} + \dfrac{1}{3}\right) + \dfrac{1}{4}$

10. $\dfrac{2}{3} + \dfrac{3}{5}$ ⬭ $\dfrac{3}{5} + \dfrac{2}{3}$

11. $1 - \dfrac{3}{5}$ ⬭ $1 - \dfrac{2}{5}$

12. $\dfrac{8}{9} - \dfrac{1}{4}$ ⬭ $\dfrac{7}{9} - \dfrac{1}{4}$

13. $\left(\dfrac{2}{5} + \dfrac{3}{4}\right) + \dfrac{1}{3}$ ⬭ $\dfrac{2}{5} + \left(\dfrac{3}{4} + \dfrac{1}{3}\right)$

14. $\dfrac{3}{4} + \dfrac{1}{8}$ ⬭ $\dfrac{1}{8} + \dfrac{3}{4}$

Write the missing number.

15. $\dfrac{3}{4} -$ ▭ $= \dfrac{3}{4}$

16. $\dfrac{1}{3} + \dfrac{1}{4} =$ ▭ $+ \dfrac{1}{3}$

17. $\dfrac{2}{3} -$ ▭ $= 0$

18. $\dfrac{3}{5} +$ ▭ $= \dfrac{3}{5}$

19. $\dfrac{5}{10} +$ ▭ $= 1$

20. $1 -$ ▭ $= \dfrac{5}{8}$

LANGUAGE OF MATHEMATICS

Write *like terms* or *unlike terms* to describe each pair of fractions.

21. $\dfrac{2}{3}$ and $\dfrac{4}{5}$ ▭

22. $\dfrac{1}{4}$ and $\dfrac{3}{4}$ ▭

23. $\dfrac{1}{7}$ and $\dfrac{5}{7}$ ▭

24. $\dfrac{3}{4}$ and $\dfrac{1}{8}$ ▭

Adding Unlike Fractions and Mixed Numbers

REACHING MY GOAL
Add unlike fractions and mixed numbers. (MA.A.3.2.3)

How did I do?

To add fractions that have unlike denominators, you first have to rename the fractions so that they have like denominators.

Example 1

Find the sum of $3\frac{2}{3}$ and $\frac{5}{6}$.

Step 1: Use a number line to estimate the sum.

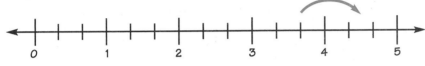

$\frac{5}{6}$ is a little less than 1, so the sum will be a little less than $4\frac{2}{3}$.

Step 2: Rename so that the fractions have the same denominator.

$$3\frac{2}{3} + \frac{5}{6} \rightarrow 3\frac{4}{6} + \frac{5}{6}$$

> **THINK**
> A common multiple of 3 and 6 is 6.

Step 3: Add the numbers.

> **Think:** To bridge from $3\frac{4}{6}$ to 4, I need to add $\frac{2}{6}$.
> I can break $\frac{5}{6}$ into $\frac{2}{6} + \frac{3}{6}$.

$$3\frac{4}{6} + \frac{5}{6} \rightarrow 3\frac{4}{6} + \frac{2}{6} + \frac{3}{6} \rightarrow 4 + \frac{3}{6} \rightarrow \boxed{}$$

Step 4: Write the answer in simplest form. Check that the answer is reasonable.

$$4\frac{3}{6} = 4\frac{1}{2}$$ $4\frac{1}{2}$ is a little less than $4\frac{2}{3}$, so the sum is reasonable.

So, $3\frac{2}{3} + \frac{5}{6} = \boxed{}$.

Example 2

Find the sum of $1\frac{3}{4}$ inches and $1\frac{1}{8}$ inches.

Step 1: Use the ruler to estimate. The sum will be a little more than $2\frac{3}{4}$ inches.

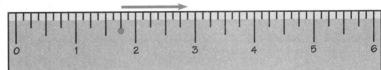

Step 2: Rename so that the fractions have the same denominator.

$$1\frac{3}{4} + 1\frac{1}{8} \rightarrow 1\frac{6}{8} + 1\frac{1}{8}$$

Step 3: Add the numbers.

$$1\frac{6}{8} + 1\frac{1}{8} = 2\frac{7}{8}$$

$2\frac{7}{8}$ is a little more than $2\frac{3}{4}$, so the sum is reasonable.

The sum of $1\frac{3}{4}$ inches and $1\frac{1}{8}$ inches is $\boxed{}$ inches.

Practice

1. Find the sum of $6\frac{3}{4}$ and $2\frac{3}{8}$.

   a. Rename so that the fractions have the same denominator.

   $6\frac{3}{4} + 2\frac{3}{8} \rightarrow 6\frac{6}{8} + 2\frac{3}{8}$

   b. Add the whole numbers.

   $6\frac{6}{8} + 2\frac{3}{8} \rightarrow 6\frac{6}{8} + 2 + \frac{3}{8} \rightarrow 8\frac{6}{8} + \frac{3}{8}$

   c. Add.

   Think: To bridge from $8\frac{6}{8}$ to 9, I need to add $\frac{2}{8}$.

   I can break $\frac{3}{8}$ into $\frac{2}{8} + \frac{1}{8}$.

   $8\frac{6}{8} + \frac{3}{8} \rightarrow 8\frac{6}{8} + \frac{2}{8} + \frac{1}{8} \rightarrow 9 + \frac{1}{8} \rightarrow 9\frac{1}{8}$

   So, $6\frac{3}{4} + 2\frac{3}{8} = $ _____.

Find the sum.

2. $\frac{3}{8} + \frac{5}{16} = $ _____

3. $\frac{3}{8} + \frac{1}{2} = $ _____

4. $\frac{4}{5} + \frac{7}{10} = $ _____

5. $\frac{5}{12} + \frac{1}{4} = $ _____

6. $\frac{7}{8} + \frac{1}{16} = $ _____

7. $\frac{2}{7} + \frac{5}{14} = $ _____

8. $9\frac{2}{5} + \frac{2}{3} = $ _____

9. $3\frac{5}{8} + \frac{3}{4} = $ _____

10. $2\frac{6}{7} + \frac{1}{3} = $ _____

11. $7\frac{4}{5} + 1\frac{1}{2} = $ _____

12. $5\frac{5}{8} + 2\frac{1}{2} = $ _____

13. $2\frac{2}{7} + 6\frac{6}{7} = $ _____

14. $3\frac{3}{4} + 2\frac{5}{8} = $ _____

15. $6\frac{4}{5} + 7\frac{7}{15} = $ _____

16. $1\frac{2}{3} + 3\frac{1}{4} = $ _____

Estimate the sum. Circle the letter of the correct answer.

17. $3\frac{7}{8} + 1\frac{1}{4} + 2\frac{3}{8}$

    A $6\frac{1}{2}$ **C** $7\frac{1}{2}$

    B $7\frac{1}{4}$ **D** $8\frac{1}{4}$

18. $2\frac{1}{8} + 3\frac{3}{8} + 4\frac{1}{16}$

    F $8\frac{5}{16}$ **H** $9\frac{5}{16}$

    G $9\frac{1}{16}$ **I** $9\frac{9}{16}$

19. $\frac{1}{8} + 1\frac{1}{4} + 1\frac{1}{8}$

    A 2   **C** 3

    B $2\frac{1}{2}$ **D** $3\frac{1}{2}$

20. $2\frac{15}{16} + \frac{7}{8} + \frac{13}{16}$

    F $3\frac{3}{4}$ **H** $4\frac{5}{8}$

    G $4\frac{3}{16}$ **I** $5\frac{1}{4}$

Problem Solving

Use the recipe to solve problems 1–6.

> **Marta's Super Sports Drink**
>
> $2\frac{1}{2}$ c orange juice $1\frac{1}{3}$ c grapefruit juice
>
> $\frac{3}{4}$ c grape juice $\frac{1}{2}$ c raspberry juice
>
> $1\frac{2}{3}$ c apple juice $\frac{1}{4}$ c lime juice
>
> $2\frac{1}{4}$ c pineapple juice $\frac{1}{8}$ c lemon juice

1. Marta mixed the orange, grape, and apple juices listed in her recipe. How many cups of juice did she have then?

2. Marta mixed the pineapple, grapefruit, and raspberry juices. What was the number of cups in that mixture?

3. Marta then combined the two mixtures. How many cups of juice were in the combined mixture?

4. Marta combined the lime juice and the lemon juice. How many cups of this mixture did she have?

5. Marta added the lemon and lime to the other juices. How many cups of her drink did she have in all?

6. Marta doubled each ingredient for another batch of her sports drink. How many cups did she use?

Solve. Write the answer in simplest form.

7. Rick has $8\frac{1}{2}$ yd of model-railroad track. He buys another $4\frac{2}{3}$ yd at the hobby shop. How many yards of track does he have now?

8. Gina has $2\frac{3}{4}$ c of flour. A recipe calls for double that amount. How much flour does the recipe call for?

9. Neil had $4\frac{1}{4}$ lb of potatoes. Jim gave him $6\frac{3}{8}$ lb more. How many pounds of potatoes did Neil have then?

10. Kelly drove $18\frac{7}{8}$ mi and stopped for lunch. After lunch, she drove $27\frac{2}{3}$ mi. How far did Kelly drive in all?

Connections

Solve. Use the table if you wish.

1. Phil put trim around the edge of a poster. He first glued 2 ft 9 in. of trim to the poster. He then glued 2 ft 6 in. of trim. What was the total length of the trim?

Equivalent Measures	
Length	**Weight**
1 ft = 12 in. 1 yd = 3 ft	1 lb = 16 oz

2. Jay bought 3 lb 6 oz of potatoes. He bought more potatoes that weighed 4 lb 8 oz. What was the total weight of Jay's purchase?

3. Nita had 7 yd 9 in. of material. She bought 3 yd 24 in. more to sew a costume. What was the total length of her material?

4. Gus had to run a fence around a rectangular garden that measured 5 ft 9 in. by 1 ft 7 in. What was the total length of the fence?

5. Gia made 4 lb 10 oz of potato salad. Then she made 3 lb 4 oz more. What was the total weight of her potato salad?

6. Carl was building a walkway. By noon, the walk was 5 ft 9 in. long. Carl finished the walk by laying 54 in. more. How long was the walkway?

7. Lucy had knitted 32 in. of a muffler. She then knitted 3 ft 10 in. to complete the muffler. What was the total length of the completed muffler?

ALGEBRA READINESS

Find the rule, and complete the function table.

8.

In	$\frac{7}{8}$	$\frac{1}{2}$	$1\frac{3}{4}$
Out	$1\frac{5}{8}$	$1\frac{1}{4}$	

Rule:

9.

In	$2\frac{2}{3}$	$4\frac{5}{6}$	$6\frac{1}{3}$
Out	3	$5\frac{1}{6}$	

Rule:

Subtracting Unlike Fractions and Mixed Numbers

REACHING MY GOAL
Subtract numbers with different denominators. (MA.A.3.2.1)

How did I do?

To subtract numbers with different denominators, you first need to rename one or both numbers so that they have the same denominator.

Example 1

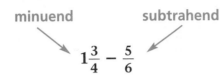

Find the difference. $1\frac{3}{4} - \frac{5}{6}$

Step 1: Rename both fractional parts so that they have the same denominator.

$$\frac{3}{4} \rightarrow \frac{3 \times 3}{4 \times 3} = \frac{9}{12} \qquad \frac{5}{6} \rightarrow \frac{5 \times \boxed{}}{6 \times \boxed{}} = \frac{10}{12}$$

Step 2: Separate the subtrahend into parts that make subtraction easy.

$$1\frac{9}{12} - \frac{10}{12} \rightarrow 1\frac{9}{12} - \frac{9}{12} - \frac{1}{12}$$

Step 3: Subtract the first part of the subtrahend.

$$(1\frac{9}{12} - \frac{9}{12}) - \frac{1}{12}$$
$$1 \qquad - \frac{1}{12}$$

> **THINK**
> Subtracting $\frac{9}{12}$ will bridge to a whole number. Then there is $\frac{1}{12}$ more to subtract.

Step 4: Subtract the second part of the subtrahend.

$$1 - \frac{1}{12} = \frac{\boxed{}}{12}$$

Example 2

$3\frac{1}{2} - 1\frac{3}{4} = ?$

Step 1: Rename the fractional part of the minuend.

$$\frac{1}{2} \rightarrow \frac{1 \times 2}{2 \times 2} = \frac{\boxed{}}{\boxed{}}$$

Step 2: Separate the subtrahend into a whole number and a fraction.

$$3\frac{2}{4} - 1\frac{3}{4} \rightarrow 3\frac{2}{4} - 1 - \frac{3}{4}$$

Step 3: Subtract the whole number.

$$(3\frac{2}{4} - 1) - \frac{3}{4}$$
$$\boxed{}\frac{2}{4} - \frac{3}{4}$$

Step 4: Subtract the fraction.

$$2\frac{2}{4} - \frac{3}{4}$$
$$2\frac{2}{4} - \frac{2}{4} - \frac{\boxed{}}{4}$$
$$2 - \frac{1}{4} = 1\frac{\boxed{}}{4}$$

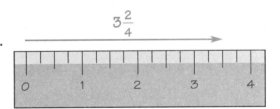

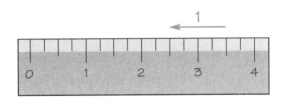

Practice

Find the difference.

1. $3\frac{3}{8} - \frac{13}{16}$

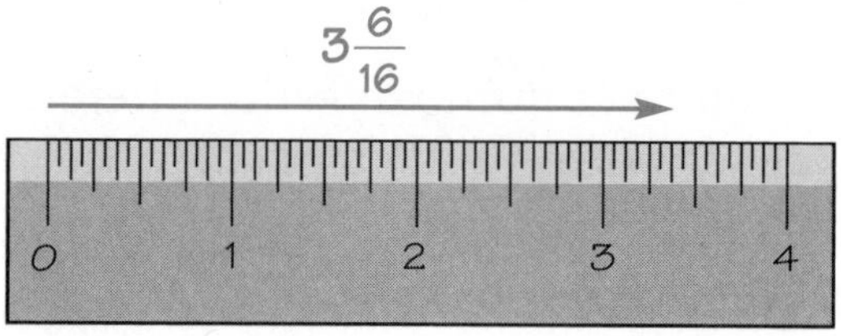

a. Rename the fractional part of the minuend.

$\frac{3}{8} \rightarrow \frac{3 \times \square}{8 \times \square} = \frac{\square}{16}$

b. Separate the subtrahend into parts that make subtraction easy.

$3\frac{6}{16} - \frac{\square}{16} - \frac{\square}{16}$

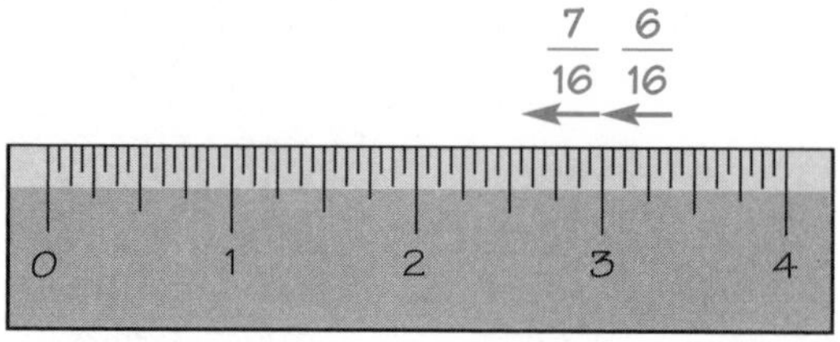

c. Subtract.

$(3\frac{6}{16} - \frac{6}{16}) - \frac{\square}{16}$

$3 - \frac{\square}{16} = 2\frac{\square}{16}$

2. $2\frac{1}{4} - \frac{4}{5}$

a. $\frac{1}{4} \rightarrow \frac{1 \times 5}{4 \times 5} = \frac{\square}{20}$

$\frac{4}{5} \rightarrow \frac{4 \times \square}{5 \times \square} = \frac{\square}{20}$

b. $2\frac{5}{20} - \frac{\square}{20} - \frac{\square}{20}$

$2 - \frac{\square}{20} = 1\frac{\square}{20}$

3. $5\frac{2}{9} - 2\frac{2}{3}$

a. $\frac{2}{3} \rightarrow \frac{2 \times \square}{3 \times \square} = \frac{\square}{9}$

b. $5\frac{2}{9} - 2 - \frac{\square}{9}$

$3\frac{2}{9} - \frac{\square}{9}$

$3\frac{2}{9} - \frac{2}{9} - \frac{\square}{9}$

$3 - \frac{\square}{9} = \square\frac{\square}{9}$

4. $4\frac{3}{10} - 1\frac{1}{2}$ $\square$

5. $7\frac{7}{8} - 3\frac{1}{4}$ $\square$

6. $10\frac{1}{6} - \frac{1}{3}$ $\square$

7. $5\frac{2}{7} - 2\frac{2}{3}$ $\square$

8. $6\frac{1}{2} - 4\frac{3}{5}$ $\square$

9. $1\frac{5}{16} - \frac{3}{4}$ $\square$

Circle the letter of the correct answer.

10. $5\frac{3}{4} - 2\frac{7}{8}$

F $2\frac{1}{8}$ **H** $3\frac{1}{8}$

G $2\frac{7}{8}$ **I** $3\frac{7}{8}$

11. $7\frac{1}{2} - 5\frac{9}{10}$

A $1\frac{3}{5}$ **C** $2\frac{3}{5}$

B $2\frac{2}{5}$ **D** $2\frac{4}{5}$

Problem Solving

Use the clues to complete the map. Then solve the problems.

- The distance from Deep Hole to Sunny Marsh, walking by Rocky Beach, is $4\frac{1}{10}$ miles.
- The distance from Sunny Marsh to Shady Rock, walking by Dirt Camp, is $6\frac{1}{2}$ miles.
- The total distance around Fish Lake is $15\frac{1}{2}$ miles.

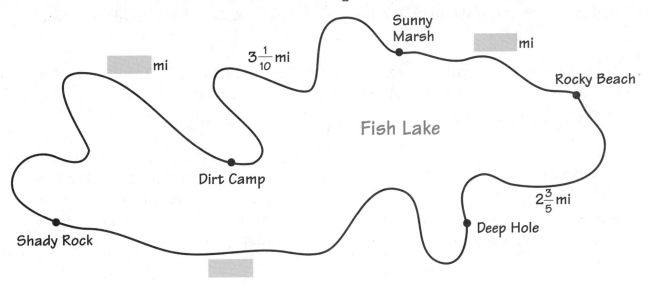

Circle the letter of the correct answer.

1. What is the distance from Deep Hole to Dirt Camp, walking by Shady Rock?

    A $7\frac{3}{10}$ mi   **C** $8\frac{3}{10}$ mi

    B $7\frac{3}{5}$ mi   **D** $8\frac{3}{5}$ mi

2. If you walk $\frac{7}{10}$ mi from Sunny Marsh toward Rocky Beach, how much farther is the beach?

    F $\frac{4}{5}$ mi   **H** $\frac{1}{2}$ mi

    G $\frac{3}{4}$ mi   **I** $\frac{2}{5}$ mi

3. If you walk $2\frac{3}{4}$ mi from Deep Hole toward Shady Rock, how much farther is the rock?

    A $1\frac{3}{20}$ mi   **C** $1\frac{1}{4}$ mi

    B $2\frac{3}{20}$ mi   **D** $2\frac{1}{4}$ mi

4. What is the distance from Rocky Beach to Shady Rock, walking by Sunny Marsh?

    F 7 mi   **H** $8\frac{1}{10}$ mi

    G 8 mi   **I** $8\frac{1}{5}$ mi

5. If you walk $1\frac{1}{2}$ mi from Dirt Camp toward Sunny Marsh, how much farther is the marsh?

    A $1\frac{3}{10}$ mi   **C** $1\frac{1}{2}$ mi

    B $1\frac{2}{5}$ mi   **D** $1\frac{3}{5}$ mi

6. Which is the shortest path from Dirt Camp to Deep Hole?

    F walking by Sunny Marsh

    G walking by Shady Rock

Connections

Use mental math to solve.

1. A book cost $9.75, and the tax was $0.50. What was the total cost?

2. The total cost of Marie's purchase was $14.20. The price of the item was $12.60. How much was the tax?

3. Daniel bought items with these prices: $8.75, $3.75, $11.80, and $4.30. Not including the tax, how much did he pay?

4. The total cost of Mr. Davis's purchase was $43.10. He returned an item that cost $5.60. What was his new total cost?

5. Michelle is 6 ft 1 in. tall. Her brother is 5 ft 10 in. tall. How much taller is Michelle than her brother?

6. Escaping a hungry tiger, Paul jumped $15\frac{1}{4}$ ft, $16\frac{1}{2}$ ft, and $14\frac{3}{4}$ ft. How far did he jump altogether?

7. Mrs. Berner bought a rug that was 9 ft 5 in. wide. The room in which she wants to put the rug is 7 ft 7 in. wide. How much does she need to cut off the rug?

8. On tiptoe, Charles can reach 5 ft 8 in. high. If he stands on a chair that is 2 ft 6 in. tall, can he reach cookies on a shelf that is 8 ft high?

9. The mass of one pumpkin is 24.8 kg. The mass of another pumpkin is 2.3 kg. What is their total mass?

10. Before a cycling vacation, Robert's mass was 49.6 kg. After the vacation, his mass was 47.9 kg. How much mass did he lose?

11. Ellen drank $3\frac{3}{4}$ cups of water. Phoebe drank $6\frac{1}{4}$ cups of water. How much more water did Phoebe drink than Ellen?

12. To make a punch, Roger mixed $3\frac{1}{2}$ cups of broccoli juice, $1\frac{3}{4}$ cups of mushroom juice, and $4\frac{3}{4}$ cups of spinach juice. How much punch did he make?

ALGEBRA READINESS

Write the 7th number in the pattern. Write the first whole number in the pattern.

13. $1\frac{3}{8}, 2\frac{3}{4}, 4\frac{1}{8}, 5\frac{1}{2} \ldots$

14. $1\frac{2}{5}, 2\frac{4}{5}, 4\frac{1}{5}, 5\frac{3}{5} \ldots$

15. $1\frac{5}{6}, 3\frac{2}{3}, 5\frac{1}{2}, 7\frac{1}{3} \ldots$

Computing with Fractions, Decimals, and Percents

REACHING MY GOAL
Solve problems involving addition and subtraction of numbers in different forms. (MA.A.3.2.3)

How did I do?

If a problem includes numbers that are in different forms, first rename all the numbers in one form.

Example 1

Jody and Sabina are camping. The map says that the trail from their camp to Harterday Falls is $5\frac{3}{4}$ miles. On their hike, they see the sign below. **How far have they hiked?**

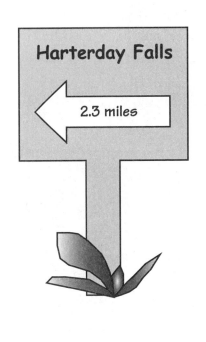

Jody's Solution

Rename the mixed number as a decimal.

$5\frac{3}{4} - 2.3$ → $5.75 - 2.3 = 3.\boxed{}$ mi

Sabina's Solution

Rename the decimal as a mixed number.

$5\frac{3}{4} - 2.3$ → $5\frac{3}{4} - 2\frac{3}{10}$

$5\frac{15}{20} - 2\frac{\boxed{}}{20}$

$5\frac{15}{20} - 2 - \frac{\boxed{}}{20}$

$\boxed{}\frac{15}{20} - \frac{\boxed{}}{20}$

$\boxed{}\frac{}{20}$mi

So, they have hiked $3.\boxed{}$ miles, or $3\frac{\boxed{}}{20}$ miles.

Example 2

There were three candidates for fifth-grade president. Lennox got 15 of the 60 votes. Sue got 35% of the votes. Chris got the rest of the votes. **Who won the election?**

Think: Percents are easy to compare. I'll rename the fraction as a percent. Then I can find the missing number and compare all three of the numbers.

Lennox's Results	**Sue's Results**	**Chris's Results**
$\frac{15}{60} = \frac{1}{4}$ → 25%	35%	$100\% - 25\% - 35\% = \boxed{}\%$

$25\% < 35\%$ $\bigcirc$ $\boxed{}\%$

So, $\boxed{}$ won the election.

Practice

1. Mr. Park has an empty flower pot that weighs $4\frac{1}{4}$ lb. He puts 10.5 lb of soil into the pot. Then he adds $2\frac{4}{5}$ lb of compost. How much does the full pot weigh?

Solution Method 1

Rename the decimal as a fraction.

$$10.5 \rightarrow 10\frac{1}{2}$$

Rewrite the fractional parts of the numbers so that they have the same denominator.

$$\frac{1}{4} \rightarrow \frac{\boxed{}}{20}$$

$$\frac{1}{2} \rightarrow \frac{\boxed{}}{20}$$

$$\frac{4}{5} \rightarrow \frac{\boxed{}}{20}$$

Add.

$$4\frac{5}{20} + 10\frac{\boxed{}}{20} + 2\frac{\boxed{}}{20} = 17\frac{\boxed{}}{20}$$

So, the full pot weighs $17\frac{\boxed{}}{20}$ lb.

Solution Method 2

Rename the fractions as decimals.

$$\frac{1}{4} \rightarrow 0.\boxed{}$$

So the decimal is 4.$\boxed{}$.

$$\frac{4}{5} \rightarrow \frac{4 \times 2}{5 \times 2} \rightarrow \frac{\boxed{}}{} = 0.\boxed{}$$

So the decimal is 2.$\boxed{}$.

Add.

$$\begin{array}{r} 4.\boxed{} \\ 2.\boxed{} \\ + 10.5 \\ \hline 17.\boxed{} \end{array}$$

So, the full pot weighs 17.$\boxed{}$ lb.

Which solution method did you find easier? Explain.

Find the sum or the difference.

2. $5.5 - 1\frac{3}{4}$

3. $15\% + 0.6 + \frac{1}{5}$

4. $\frac{9}{10} - 0.75 - 10\%$

5. $8.5 + 2\frac{1}{4} + \frac{1}{2}$

6. $80\% - 0.49 - 1\%$

7. $10.35 + \frac{4}{25}$

8. $1\frac{3}{5} - \frac{3}{10} - 0.9$

9. $23\frac{1}{4} + 12.75$

10. $1 - 14\% - \frac{17}{20}$

A percent is a fraction with a denominator of 100. Could you write a mixed number such as $1\frac{1}{2}$ as a percent? How?

Problem Solving

✦✧ Sum of One ✧✦

The Fabulous New Board Game from the Makers of Double-Halve-Double! Great for Parties!

Rules for One Player

- The object is to choose one number from each column to get a sum of 1.

- Use each number once. Cross a number out when it has been used.

- Continue until all the numbers have been used. You should find six sums of 1.

Rules for Two Players

- The object is to get the highest sum equal to 1 or less than 1, but *not* more than 1.

- The numbers of both players are added in the same sum.

- Players take turns choosing numbers.

- Numbers are chosen from columns, in order: Column 1, Column 2, Column 3, Column 1, and so on.

- When a player cannot choose a number without exceeding the sum of 1, the other player wins the round. The player who lost begins the new round.

Sample Play
Player 1 picks $\frac{11}{50}$ from Column 1.
Player 2 picks 0.51 from Column 2. The sum is 0.73.
Player 1 picks 25% from Column 3. The sum is 0.98.
Player 2 cannot pick a number from Column 1 without exceeding the sum of 1. Player 1 wins the round.
Player 2 picks a new number from Column 1.

Column 1	Column 2	Column 3
$\frac{7}{25}$	0.35	48%
$\frac{11}{50}$	0.3	5%
$\frac{2}{5}$	0.15	25%
$\frac{2}{25}$	0.1	21%
$\frac{17}{20}$	0.51	52%
$\frac{23}{50}$	0.4	39%

Connections

Solve.

1. Paul is $6\frac{1}{2}$ ft tall. Robert is 5 ft 10 in. tall. How much shorter is Robert than Paul?

2. If you travel $2\frac{3}{4}$ hours by train, 45 minutes by car, and 20 minutes by foot, how long have you traveled altogether?

3. Melisa ate a hamburger that weighed $1\frac{1}{8}$ lb. Angie ate a hamburger that weighed 10 oz. How much more did Melisa's hamburger weigh than Angie's?

4. A cricket walked 18 in. north. Then it walked $\frac{2}{3}$ ft. south. Finally, it walked 6 in. north again. How far was the cricket from its starting point?

5. Two friends went to the movies together, but saw different movies. The older friend's movie started at 2:15 P.M. and lasted for 1 hour 55 minutes. The younger friend's movie started at 1:50 P.M. and lasted for $2\frac{1}{2}$ hours. Which friend had to wait afterward, and for how long?

6. A box can hold 20 lb. A man puts two objects into the box. The first object weighs $6\frac{3}{4}$ lb, and the second object weighs 9 lb 11 oz. Can the box hold a third object that weighs $3\frac{1}{2}$ lb?

To study the health of a stream, a scientist caught, measured, and released some trout. **Use her stem-and-leaf plot to answer the questions.**

Length of Trout (inches)

2	0 2 4 4 5
1	0 1 1 2 2 4 5 7 8
0	5 6 6 7 9 9

7. What percent of the trout caught were less than 9 in. long?

8. What percent of the trout caught were more than 12 in. long?

9. What percent of the trout caught were more than $1\frac{1}{2}$ ft and less than 2 ft in length?

10. What percent of the trout caught were less than 10 in. long?

11. What percent of the trout caught were more than 7 in. long?

12. What percent of the trout caught were more than $\frac{1}{2}$ ft and less than $1\frac{1}{2}$ ft in length?

Finding a Fraction of a Number

REACHING MY GOAL
Use models and multiplication to find fractions of whole numbers. (MA.A.3.2.1)

How did I do?

A. You can use a model to find a fraction of a number.

Example 1

Antony recorded 20 songs for a new CD, and played guitar on $\frac{1}{4}$ of them. On how many songs did Antony play guitar?

Step 1: Draw a model showing 20 songs.

Step 2: To find $\frac{1}{4}$ of the songs, divide the total number into 4 equal groups.

$20 \div 4 = 5$ So, $\frac{1}{4}$ of 20 = 5.

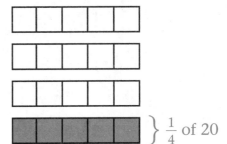

Antony played guitar on ⬜ songs.

Example 2

Julia played drums on $\frac{3}{4}$ of the 20 songs on Antony's CD. On how many songs did she play drums?

Step 1: Find $\frac{1}{4}$ of 20.

$20 \div 4 = 5$ So, $\frac{1}{4}$ of 20 = 5.

Step 2: Find $\frac{3}{4}$ of 20.

Think: $\frac{3}{4}$ is the same as $3 \times \frac{1}{4}$.

So, $\frac{3}{4} \times 20 \rightarrow 3 \times \frac{1}{4}$ of 20.

$3 \times 5 =$ ⬜

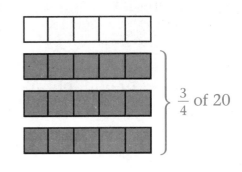

Julia played drums on ⬜ songs.

B. You can multiply to find a fraction of a number.

Example 3

Find $\frac{1}{4}$ of 12.

$\frac{1}{4} \times 12 \rightarrow \frac{1 \times 12}{4} \rightarrow \frac{12}{4}$ Simplify: $\frac{12}{4} \rightarrow 12 \div 4 =$ ⬜

Example 4

Find $\frac{3}{4}$ of 2.

$\frac{3}{4} \times 2 \rightarrow \frac{3 \times 2}{4} \rightarrow \frac{6}{4}$ Simplify: $\frac{6}{4} \rightarrow 1\frac{2}{4} = 1\frac{\ }{\ }$

Practice

1. Find $\frac{2}{3}$ of the 15 squares in the box.

   a. Divide 15 into 3 equal parts. Each of the 3 parts has [ ] boxes. Shade 2 of the parts.

   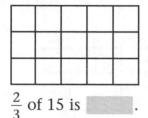

   $\frac{2}{3}$ of 15 is [ ].

   b. Use multiplication.

   $\frac{2}{3} \times 15 \rightarrow \frac{2 \times 15}{3} \rightarrow \frac{30}{3}$

   $\frac{30}{3} \rightarrow 30 \div 3 =$ [ ]

2. Find $\frac{2}{3}$ of 4.

   Use multiplication.

   $\frac{2}{3} \times 4 \rightarrow \frac{2 \times 4}{3} \rightarrow \frac{}{} = \boxed{}\frac{}{}$

3. Find $\frac{1}{5}$ of 6.

   Use multiplication.

   $\frac{1}{5} \times 6 \rightarrow \frac{1 \times 6}{5} \rightarrow \frac{}{} = \boxed{}\frac{}{}$

> **THINK**
> When the denominator of the fraction isn't a factor of the whole number, it's easier to multiply than to use a model.

Use a model or multiplication to find each value. Simplify.

4. $\frac{1}{2}$ of 12 [ ]

5. $\frac{1}{3}$ of 4 [ ]

6. $\frac{2}{7}$ of 14 [ ]

7. $\frac{1}{4}$ of 28 [ ]

8. $\frac{5}{8}$ of 8 [ ]

9. $\frac{3}{4}$ of 6 [ ]

10. $\frac{2}{5}$ of 9 [ ]

11. $\frac{4}{9}$ of 18 [ ]

12. $\frac{5}{6}$ of 36 [ ]

13. $\frac{2}{3}$ of 5 [ ]

14. $\frac{2}{3}$ of 2 [ ]

15. $\frac{4}{10}$ of 5 [ ]

16. $\frac{1}{2}$ of 5 [ ]

17. $\frac{1}{10}$ of 13 [ ]

18. $\frac{5}{12}$ of 10 [ ]

Circle the letter of the correct choice.

19. On a school bus one morning, $\frac{2}{5}$ of the passengers were boys. There were 35 passengers on the bus. How many of them were boys?

    A 10   C 21

    B 14   D 33

20. Grace Ann has 16 nature books, and $\frac{1}{4}$ of them are about sea creatures. How many of Grace Ann's nature books are *not* about sea creatures?

    F 16   H 8

    G 12   I 4

Problem Solving

Jerry spent $24 this week. His expenditures are shown in the circle graph.
Use the graph to solve problems 1–4.

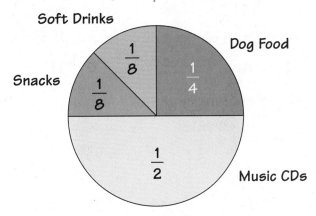

Jerry's Expenditures

1. How much money did Jerry spend on dog food this week?

2. How much money did Jerry spend on music CDs this week?

3. What is the total amount that Jerry spent on snacks and soft drinks?

4. How much more did Jerry spend on music CDs than on snacks?

The 30 students in Mrs. Johnson's class listed their favorite pets. Their choices are shown in the circle graph. **Use the graph to solve problems 5–8.**

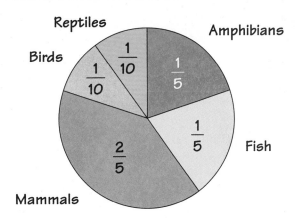

Favorite Pets in Mrs. Johnson's Class

5. How many students chose mammals as their favorite pet?

6. How many more students chose amphibians as their favorite pet than chose reptiles?

7. What is the total number of students who chose either birds or fish?

8. Together, which three types of pets were chosen by $\frac{4}{5}$ of the class?

Connections

Circle the letter of the correct answer.

1. It took Sami $\frac{3}{4}$ of an hour to clean his room. For how many minutes did he clean the room?

   A 30 min   **C** 40 min

   B 35 min   **D** 45 min

2. It took Gina $\frac{1}{5}$ of an hour to walk to school. For how many minutes did she walk?

   F 50 min   **H** 15 min

   G 20 min   **I** 12 min

3. Paul bought $\frac{3}{4}$ pound of provolone cheese. How many ounces of cheese did he buy?

   A 3 oz   **C** 9 oz

   B 4 oz   **D** 12 oz

4. Ann accidentally broke her 1-foot ruler, and now it's only $\frac{2}{3}$ of its original length. How long is the ruler?

   F 9 in.   **H** 6 in.

   G 8 in.   **I** 4 in.

5. Josepha has a silver bowl that weighs $\frac{3}{8}$ pound. How many ounces of silver does she have?

   A 3 oz   **C** 8 oz

   B 6 oz   **D** 12 oz

6. Al used $\frac{5}{6}$ yard of red ribbon to decorate a present. How many inches of ribbon did he use?

   F 6 in.   **H** 30 in.

   G 10 in.   **I** 36 in.

7. In the rectangle below, region A takes up $\frac{1}{2}$ of the area, region B takes up $\frac{1}{3}$ of the area, and region C takes up $\frac{1}{6}$ of the area. Find the area of each region.

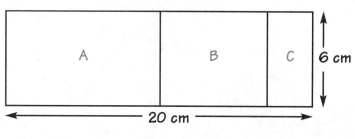

region A [ ]   region B [ ]   region C [ ]

8. In the rectangle below, region L takes up $\frac{1}{4}$ of the area, region M takes up $\frac{5}{8}$ of the area, and region N takes up $\frac{1}{8}$ of the area. Find the area of each region.

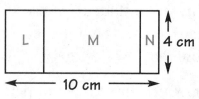

region L [ ]   region M [ ]   region N [ ]

Multiplying Whole Numbers and Fractions

REACHING MY GOAL
Multiply whole numbers and fractions. (MA.A.3.2.1)

How did I do?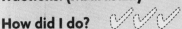

You can use a number line or addition to help you multiply fractions.

Example 1

Venice is going to bake 6 pies. Each pie requires $\frac{1}{4}$ cup of flour. How many cups of flour does she need?

a. Use a number line to find 6 fourths:

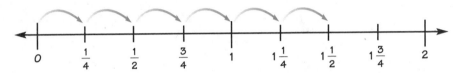

b. Add 6 fourths to find the total:

$$\frac{1}{4} + \frac{1}{4} + \frac{1}{4} + \frac{1}{4} + \frac{1}{4} + \frac{1}{4} = \frac{6}{4}$$ Simplify: $\frac{6}{4} \rightarrow \frac{3}{2} \rightarrow 1\frac{\boxed{}}{2}$

c. Or find the answer by multiplication:

$$6 \times \frac{1}{4} \rightarrow \frac{6 \times 1}{4} \rightarrow \frac{6}{4}$$ Simplify: $\frac{6}{4} \rightarrow \frac{3}{2} \rightarrow 1\frac{\boxed{}}{2}$

Venice needs ____ cups of flour.

Example 2

Venice will use $\frac{3}{4}$ cup strawberries in each of the 6 pies. How many cups of strawberries does she need?

a. Use a number line:

b. Add:

$$\frac{3}{4} + \frac{3}{4} + \frac{3}{4} + \frac{3}{4} + \frac{3}{4} + \frac{3}{4} = \frac{\boxed{}}{4}$$ Simplify: $\frac{\boxed{}}{4} \rightarrow \boxed{}\frac{\boxed{}}{2}$

c. Multiply:

$$6 \times \frac{3}{4} = \frac{6 \times 3}{4} \rightarrow \frac{\boxed{}}{4}$$ Simplify: $\frac{\boxed{}}{4} \rightarrow \boxed{}\frac{\boxed{}}{2}$

So, Venice needs ____ cups of strawberries.

Practice

Each number line shows multiplication of a fraction or mixed number.
Complete the addition and multiplication sentences to solve the problem shown on the number line.

1.

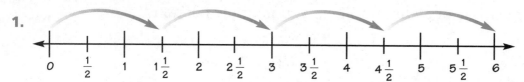

Add: $\quad 1\frac{1}{2} + 1\frac{1}{2} + 1\frac{1}{2} + 1\frac{1}{2} = $ ▢

Add: $\quad \frac{3}{2} + \frac{3}{2} + \frac{3}{2} + \frac{3}{2} \rightarrow \dfrac{▢}{2} = $ ▢

Multiply: ▢ $\times \dfrac{3}{2} \rightarrow \dfrac{▢}{2} = $ ▢

2.

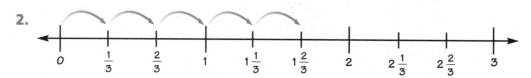

Add: $\quad \dfrac{▢}{▢} + \dfrac{▢}{▢} + \dfrac{▢}{▢} + \dfrac{▢}{▢} + \dfrac{▢}{▢} \rightarrow \dfrac{▢}{▢} = $ ▢

Multiply: ▢ $\times \dfrac{1}{3} \rightarrow \dfrac{▢}{3} = $ ▢

Solve, writing the answer in simplest form. Use the number line if you like.

3. $7 \times \dfrac{1}{5} = $ ▢

4. $4 \times \dfrac{1}{2} = $ ▢

5. $3 \times \dfrac{5}{6} = $ ▢

6. $4 \times \dfrac{2}{3} = $ ▢

Multiply. Write the answer in simplest form.

7. $5 \times \dfrac{1}{6} = $ ▢

8. $5 \times \dfrac{2}{6} = $ ▢

9. $4 \times \dfrac{3}{5} = $ ▢

10. $8 \times \dfrac{3}{4} = $ ▢

11. $2 \times 1\dfrac{1}{2} = $ ▢

12. $7 \times \dfrac{2}{5} = $ ▢

13. $3 \times 1\dfrac{1}{4} = $ ▢

14. $10 \times \dfrac{2}{3} = $ ▢

Problem Solving

Solve. Write the answer in simplest form.

1. Giselle needs $\frac{3}{4}$ cup of sugar to make a batch of cookies. She plans to make 6 batches. How many cups of sugar does she need?

2. The distance from Mark's house to the bank is 6 miles. He has driven $\frac{3}{4}$ of the way. How many miles has he driven?

3. Kent pours $\frac{2}{3}$ cup of lemonade into each glass. There are 9 glasses in all. How many cups of lemonade does Kent use?

4. There are 9 students in Charlotte's group. On Monday, $\frac{2}{3}$ of the students go to band practice. How many students go to band practice?

5. Each pack of cheese is $\frac{1}{2}$ pound. Margery bought 7 packs. How many pounds of cheese did she buy?

6. Edgar is riding his bike 7 miles to a friend's house. He is halfway there. How many miles has he biked?

7. Andy exercises for $\frac{1}{3}$ hour, 4 times a week. How many hours does he exercise each week?

8. A container can hold 4 gallons. If the container is $\frac{1}{3}$ full of water, how many gallons of water are in it?

9. A company ships 60 boxes. Each box weighs $\frac{5}{6}$ pound. What is the total weight of the boxes?

10. How many minutes are in $\frac{5}{6}$ of an hour?

11. Compare your answers in the left column to those in the right column, and make a general statement about multiplication.

When you multiply fractions and whole numbers, changing the order of the factors _____ change the product.

Connections

Use the formula $A = \frac{1}{2} \cdot (b \times h)$ to find the area of the triangle.
Write the answer in simplest form.

1.

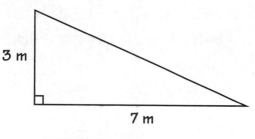

area:

2.

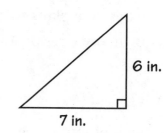

area:

3.

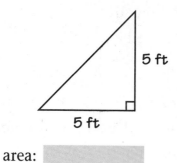

area:

4.

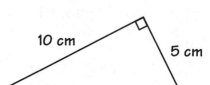

area:

Find the perimeter of the regular figure. Write the answer in simplest form.

5.

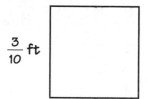

$\frac{3}{10}$ ft

perimeter:

6.

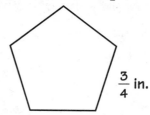

$\frac{3}{4}$ in.

perimeter:

7.

$\frac{1}{6}$ ft

perimeter:

8.

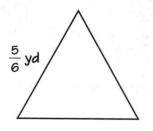

$\frac{5}{6}$ yd

perimeter:

ALGEBRA READINESS

Compare. Write <, >, or =.

9. $6 \times \frac{1}{8}$ ⬭ $\frac{1}{8} \times 6$

10. $5 \times \frac{1}{4}$ ⬭ $6 \times \frac{1}{4}$

11. $3 \times \frac{3}{10}$ ⬭ $9 \times \frac{1}{10}$

12. $7 \times \frac{1}{4}$ ⬭ $\frac{7}{5}$

13. $\frac{3}{4}$ of 8 ⬭ 8

14. $\frac{2}{3}$ of 5 ⬭ $\frac{2}{3} \times 10$

• TOPIC 6: Fractions, Mixed Numbers, and Percent Lesson 22

Multiplying by a Fraction

REACHING MY GOAL
Multiply fractions using drawings and algorithms. (MA.A.3.2.1)

How did I do?

A. You can use a model to find the product of fractions.

Example 1

Stan has $\frac{3}{5}$ pound of bronze. He uses half of it to make a small sculpture. How much does the sculpture weigh?

Think: To solve the problem, you must find $\frac{1}{2}$ of $\frac{3}{5}$.

Step 1: Draw a rectangle, and divide it into fifths. Shade 3 parts to show $\frac{3}{5}$.

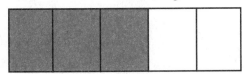

Step 2: Divide the model horizontally into halves. Shade one half. The part that you have shaded twice is $\frac{1}{2}$ of $\frac{3}{5}$.

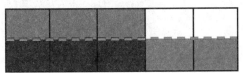

> **THINK**
> There are 10 parts in all.
> 3 of them are shaded twice.

So, the sculpture weighs $\frac{}{10}$ pound.

B. You can also find the product of two fractions by using multiplication.

Example 2

Find $\frac{5}{6} \times \frac{3}{4}$.

Step 1: Multiply the numerators and then multiply the denominators.

$$\frac{5}{6} \times \frac{3}{4} \rightarrow \frac{5 \times 3}{6 \times 4} = \frac{}{24}$$

Step 2: Simplify, if necessary.

$$\frac{}{24} = \frac{}{8}$$

So, $\frac{5}{6} \times \frac{3}{4} = \frac{}{8}$.

Practice

1. Fiona has $\frac{1}{4}$ yard of silver chain. She uses $\frac{2}{3}$ of it for a bracelet. How many yards long is the bracelet?

   a. Shade 1 of 4 parts in the model to show $\frac{1}{4}$.

   b. Divide the model into thirds. Shade two thirds.

   c. Count the parts that are shaded twice. $\frac{\boxed{}}{12}$

   Simplify. $\frac{\boxed{}}{12} = \frac{\boxed{}}{\boxed{}}$

   The bracelet is $\boxed{}$ yard long.

Multiply. Write the answer in simplest form.

2. $\frac{1}{8} \times \frac{1}{4} = \boxed{}$

3. $\frac{3}{8} \times \frac{1}{3} = \boxed{}$

4. $\frac{1}{3} \times \frac{1}{3} = \boxed{}$

5. $\frac{4}{5} \times \frac{1}{3} = \boxed{}$

6. $\frac{5}{8} \times \frac{2}{5} = \boxed{}$

7. $\frac{7}{12} \times \frac{1}{7} = \boxed{}$

8. $4 \times \frac{3}{5} = \boxed{}$

9. $\frac{1}{3} \times 2 = \boxed{}$

10. $\frac{3}{8} \times 4 = \boxed{}$

11. $6 \times \frac{1}{6} = \boxed{}$

12. $\frac{4}{5} \times 2 = \boxed{}$

13. $2 \times \frac{7}{8} = \boxed{}$

14. Now make some general statements. Write *sometimes*, *always*, or *never*.

   If fractions are less than 1,
   - the product of two fractions is $\boxed{}$ less than 1.
   - the product of two fractions is $\boxed{}$ less than either fraction.
   - the product of a fraction and a whole number is $\boxed{}$ less than 1.
   - the product of a fraction and a whole number is $\boxed{}$ less than the whole number.

Compare. Write <, >, or =.

15. $\frac{2}{3} \times \frac{1}{2} \enspace \bigcirc \enspace \frac{1}{2} \times \frac{3}{4}$

16. $\frac{3}{4} \times \frac{5}{8} \enspace \bigcirc \enspace \frac{3}{4}$

17. $\frac{1}{5} \enspace \bigcirc \enspace \frac{2}{3} \times \frac{1}{5}$

18. $\frac{1}{4} \times 4 \enspace \bigcirc \enspace 5 \times \frac{1}{5}$

19. $\frac{11}{12} \times \frac{7}{8} \enspace \bigcirc \enspace 1$

20. $16 \enspace \bigcirc \enspace \frac{9}{10} \times 16$

Problem Solving

Circle the letter of the correct answer.

1. Mina uses $\frac{1}{6}$ of the sugar in a container that holds $\frac{2}{3}$ cups. How many cups of sugar did she use?

   A $\frac{1}{9}$ cup   **C** $\frac{1}{3}$ cup

   B $\frac{1}{6}$ cup   **D** $\frac{1}{2}$ cup

2. Dale must walk $\frac{4}{5}$ of a mile to school. If he is halfway to school, how far has he walked?

   F $\frac{1}{3}$ mile   **H** $\frac{1}{2}$ mile

   G $\frac{2}{5}$ mile   **I** $\frac{4}{5}$ mile

3. Virginia spends about $\frac{1}{3}$ of each 24-hour day at school. About how many hours is she at school?

   A 3 hours   **C** 6 hours

   B 4 hours   **D** 8 hours

4. Mr. Simpson bought $\frac{1}{2}$ gallon of milk. He used $\frac{1}{4}$ of the milk to make milk shakes. How much milk is left?

   F $\frac{1}{8}$ gallon   **H** $\frac{2}{3}$ gallon

   G $\frac{3}{8}$ gallon   **I** $\frac{3}{4}$ gallon

5. Juan has a board that is $\frac{3}{4}$ foot long. He saws the board into six equal lengths. How long is each piece?

   A $\frac{1}{16}$ foot   **C** $\frac{3}{10}$ foot

   B $\frac{1}{8}$ foot   **D** $\frac{3}{8}$ foot

6. Alison has 5 pounds of flour. She uses $\frac{5}{6}$ of the flour to bake cookies. How many pounds of flour did she use?

   F $\frac{5}{6}$ lb   **H** $3\frac{1}{3}$ lb

   G $1\frac{2}{3}$ lb   **I** $4\frac{1}{6}$ lb

7. Margarita is riding her bike on a 12-mile trail. She has biked $\frac{1}{4}$ of the way. How many miles are left?

   A 3 miles   **C** 8 miles

   B 7 miles   **D** 9 miles

8. A liter bottle of juice is $\frac{3}{4}$ full. Lewis drinks $\frac{2}{3}$ of the remaining juice. How much juice did he drink?

   F $\frac{1}{3}$ liter   **H** $\frac{1}{2}$ liter

   G $\frac{5}{12}$ liter   **I** $\frac{5}{7}$ liter

9. A pan of lasagna is cut into 18 slices. At dinner, the Castiglia family eats $\frac{2}{3}$ of the lasagna. How many slices do they eat?

   A 2 slices   **C** 12 slices

   B 9 slices   **D** 16 slices

10. A pie is cut into 12 slices. After dinner, $\frac{1}{2}$ of the slices remain. The following morning, $\frac{5}{6}$ of those slices are eaten. How many slices are left?

    F 1 slice   **H** 4 slices

    G 2 slices   **I** 5 slices

> When does the product of a fraction and a whole number equal 1?

Connections

Use the diagram and the information in the box for problems 1–4.

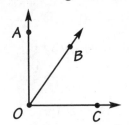

> Angle AOC is a right angle.
>
> The ratio of the measures of ∠AOB to ∠BOC is 2:3.

1. What fraction of ∠AOC does ∠AOB represent? ____

2. What fraction of ∠AOC does ∠BOC represent? ____

3. What is the measure of angle ∠AOB? ____

4. What is the measure of angle ∠BOC? ____

ALGEBRA READINESS

The rectangular field at the right was divided so that $\frac{1}{3}$ of it was a vegetable garden, and $\frac{1}{4}$ of that garden was planted with corn. How many square feet were planted with corn?

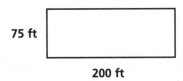

75 ft

200 ft

Angela solves the problem this way:

  a. Multiply the field's length and width to find its area.

  b. Multiply the field's area by $\frac{1}{3}$ to find the area of the garden.

  c. Multiply the garden area by $\frac{1}{4}$ to find the area planted with corn.

Brad solves the problem this way:

  a. Multiply $\frac{1}{4}$ by $\frac{1}{3}$ to find the fraction of the field that is planted with corn.

  b. Multiply the field's length and width to find its area.

  c. Multiply the field's area by the fraction that is corn to find the area of corn.

5. Will Angela, Brad, or both get the correct answer? Explain.

6. How many square feet were planted with corn? ____

LANGUAGE OF MATHEMATICS

7. Find three fourths of two thirds. ____

8. What is the product of one half and four fifths? ____

Percent of a Number

A. You can find a percent of a number. First write the percent as a fraction or as a decimal, and then multiply.

Example 1

A zookeeper gave an elephant 250 lb of food. The elephant ate only 70% of the food. **How many pounds of food did the elephant eat?**

Step 1: Write the percent as a fraction or as a decimal.

$$70\% \rightarrow \frac{70}{100} = \frac{\boxed{}}{10}$$ or $$70\% \rightarrow \frac{70}{100} = 0.\boxed{}$$

Step 2: Multiply.

$$\frac{7}{10} \times 250 \rightarrow \frac{1750}{10} = \boxed{}$$ or $$0.7 \times 250 = \boxed{}$$

So, the elephant ate $\boxed{}$ lb of food.

B. You can estimate a percent of a number by approximating the percent with a benchmark fraction.

Example 2

On a store's twenty-third anniversary, it marked all prices down 23%. **About how much will you save if you purchase a pair of shoes that originally cost $60?**

Step 1: Approximate the percent.

23% is close to 25%, which is $\frac{\boxed{}}{4}$.

Step 2: Multiply.

$$\frac{1}{4} \times \$60 = \$\boxed{}$$

So, you will save about $\$\boxed{}$.

C. Sales tax is computed as a percent of an item's price.

Example 3

A chair costs $70, and the sales tax is 8%. **How much is the sales tax?**

Step 1: Write the percent as a decimal.   8% = 0.08

Step 2: Multiply.

$$\begin{array}{r} 70 \\ \times\, 0.08 \\ \hline \boxed{} \end{array}$$

> **THINK**
> Dollars are decimal amounts, so it is easy to compute sales tax using decimals.

So, the sales tax is $\$\boxed{}$.

Practice

Find the percent of the number.

1. 30% of 40

   a. Write the percent as a fraction or decimal.

   $30\% = \dfrac{}{10}$ or $30\% = 0.\boxed{}$

   b. Multiply.

   $\dfrac{3}{10} \times 40 = \boxed{}$ or $0.3 \times 40 = \boxed{}$

2. 25% of 12 $\boxed{}$

3. 90% of 300 $\boxed{}$

4. 50% of 78 $\boxed{}$

5. 10% of 840 $\boxed{}$

6. 75% of 24 $\boxed{}$

7. 80% of 80 $\boxed{}$

Estimate the percent of the number.

8. 63% of 50

   a. Choose a benchmark. 63% is close to 60%, which is $\dfrac{}{10}$.

   b. Multiply. $\dfrac{6}{10} \times 50 \rightarrow \dfrac{\boxed{}}{10} = \boxed{}$

   So, 63% of 50 is about $\boxed{}$.

9. 47% of 38
   about $\boxed{}$

10. 12% of 170
    about $\boxed{}$

11. 74% of 4
    about $\boxed{}$

12. 31% of 200
    about $\boxed{}$

13. 26% of 480
    about $\boxed{}$

14. 89% of 70
    about $\boxed{}$

Solve.

15. The price of a book is $18. If the sales tax is 6%, what is the total cost of the book?

    a. Find the amount of the tax. $18 \times 0.\boxed{} = \boxed{}$

    b. Add the tax to the price of the book. $18 + \boxed{} = \boxed{}$

    So, the total cost of the book is $\boxed{}$.

16. Mr. Smith bought a rake for $25. If the sales tax is 7%, how much is the total cost of the rake?

    $\boxed{}$

17. Martha's drugstore purchases totaled $56.50. If the sales tax is 8%, how much was her total bill?

    $\boxed{}$

Problem Solving

A garden club raised money by selling calendars. The sales of Daisy calendars were the same percent of total sales as the sales of Lilac calendars. **Complete the graph. Use the graph to complete the table. Then answer the questions.**

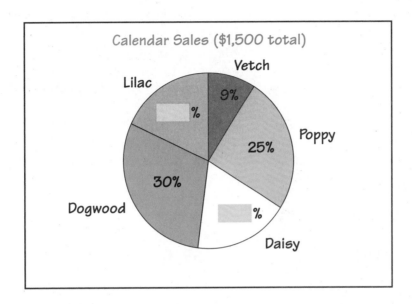

Calendar	Dollar Sales	Number of Calendars Sold	Price of 1 Calendar
Poppy	$		$15
Daisy	$	30	$
Dogwood	$		$6
Lilac	$	27	$
Vetch	$		$9

1. How many calendars were sold altogether?

2. Which calendar cost the most?

3. Did the most popular calendar have the greatest dollar sales?

4. How much would it cost to buy a set of all five calendars?

5. How much would it cost to buy a set of all five calendars with sales tax of 5%?

6. One member of the garden club sold 25% of the calendars. How many calendars did he sell?

What fraction is equivalent to $12\frac{1}{2}\%$? Explain.

Connections

Find the product.

1. 6×7.2

2. 8×2.5

3. 12×3.7

4. 4.05×70

5. 1.5×24

6. 9.12×4

7. 0.33×5

8. 16×1.75

9. 78×0.25

10. 5.7×20

ALGEBRA READINESS

Compare. Write < , >, or =.

11. 25% of 80 ⬭ 80% of 25

12. 50% of 40 ⬭ 60% of 40

13. 50% of 90 ⬭ 50% of 89

14. 25% of 4 ⬭ 1% of 100

15. 60% of 80 ⬭ 30% of 180

16. 10% of 30 ⬭ 30% of 10

LANGUAGE OF MATHEMATICS

Write the number.

17. I am a multiple of 7 that is greater than 50% of 40 but less than 50% of 50.

18. I am a prime number that is greater than the least common multiple of 6 and 8 but less than 10% of 300.

19. I am a prime number that is a factor of 99 and is more than 10% of 50.

20. I am a common factor of 24 and 36 that is less than 25% of 8.

Multiplying with Mixed Numbers

REACHING MY GOAL
Multiply fractions and whole numbers by mixed numbers.
(MA.A.3.2.1)

How did I do?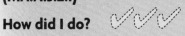

A. You can multiply a mixed number by a fraction. Draw an area model or multiply the numbers written as fractions.

Example 1

Find $\frac{2}{3} \times 2\frac{1}{4}$. Write the product in simplest form.

Step 1: Draw three squares, and divide them into quarters. Shade $2\frac{1}{4}$ squares.

Step 2: Divide the squares horizontally into thirds. Shade two thirds. The part that you have shaded twice is $\frac{2}{3}$ of $2\frac{1}{4}$.

parts shaded twice $\longrightarrow$
parts in each square $\longrightarrow$ $\frac{18}{12} = \boxed{}\frac{\boxed{}}{2}$

You can also find the product by writing the mixed number as a fraction.

Step 1: Write $2\frac{1}{4}$ as a fraction greater than 1. $2\frac{1}{4} \longrightarrow \frac{9}{4}$

Step 2: Multiply the numerators, and multiply the denominators.

$$\frac{2}{3} \times \frac{9}{4} \longrightarrow \frac{2 \times 9}{3 \times 4} = \frac{\boxed{}}{12} \longrightarrow \boxed{}\frac{\boxed{}}{2}$$

B. You can multiply a mixed number by a whole number. Draw a number line or multiply the numbers written as fractions.

Example 2

Find $3 \times 2\frac{3}{4}$. Write the product in simplest form.

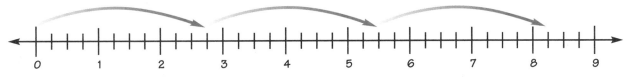

Step 1: Write both numbers as fractions greater than 1.

$$3 = \frac{3}{1} \qquad\qquad 2\frac{3}{4} = \frac{11}{4}$$

Step 2: Multiply the numerators, and multiply the denominators.

$$\frac{3}{1} \times \frac{11}{4} \longrightarrow \frac{3 \times 11}{1 \times 4} = \frac{\boxed{}}{4} \longrightarrow \boxed{}\frac{\boxed{}}{4}$$

Practice

Use the model to multiply. Write the product in simplest form.

1. Find $\frac{5}{6} \times 1\frac{1}{3}$.

← parts shaded twice
← parts in each whole

So, $\frac{5}{6} \times 1\frac{1}{3} = $ [   ].

Multiply. Write the product in simplest form.

2. $\frac{3}{5} \times 2\frac{1}{2}$

$\frac{3}{5} \times \dfrac{\boxed{}}{2} \longrightarrow \dfrac{3 \times \boxed{}}{5 \times 2} = \boxed{} \longrightarrow \boxed{}$

3. $4 \times 5\frac{2}{3}$

$\frac{4}{1} \times \boxed{} \longrightarrow \dfrac{4 \times \boxed{}}{1 \times \boxed{}} = \boxed{} \longrightarrow \boxed{}$

4. $\frac{5}{8} \times \frac{3}{4} = $ [   ]

5. $\frac{5}{6} \times 12 = $ [   ]

6. $\frac{11}{10} \times 2\frac{1}{4} = $ [   ]

7. $\frac{3}{4} \times 8\frac{1}{3} = $ [   ]

8. $1\frac{1}{2} \times 1\frac{1}{2} = $ [   ]

9. $6 \times 3\frac{2}{3} = $ [   ]

10. $\frac{1}{12} \times 2\frac{1}{4} = $ [   ]

11. $\frac{5}{8} \times 3\frac{1}{4} = $ [   ]

12. Now you can make general statements. Write *sometimes*, *always*, or *never*.

> If a fraction is less than 1:
> - the product of that fraction and a mixed number is [   ] less than 1.
> - the product of that fraction and a mixed number is [   ] less than the mixed number.

Circle the letter of the correct answer.

13. What is $\frac{3}{4}$ of $8\frac{1}{2}$?

    A $4\frac{1}{4}$ **C** $12\frac{3}{4}$

    B $6\frac{3}{8}$ **D** 51

14. What is the product of $5\frac{1}{3}$ and $1\frac{1}{4}$?

    F $6\frac{2}{3}$ **H** $6\frac{1}{12}$

    G $6\frac{1}{4}$ **I** $2\frac{2}{3}$

15. What is the product of 8 and $3\frac{1}{8}$?

    A $4\frac{7}{8}$ **C** 24

    B $11\frac{1}{8}$ **D** 25

16. What is $\frac{2}{5}$ of $7\frac{3}{4}$?

    F $8\frac{1}{5}$ **H** $3\frac{1}{10}$

    G $3\frac{7}{8}$ **I** $1\frac{11}{10}$

Problem Solving

Circle the letter of the correct answer.

1. A muffin recipe calls for $1\frac{1}{4}$ teaspoons of baking powder. How many teaspoons of baking powder do you need for 5 batches of muffins?

   A 5 tsp   **C** $6\frac{1}{4}$ tsp

   B 6 tsp   **D** $12\frac{1}{2}$ tsp

2. Giancarlo is shipping two packages. One package weighs $3\frac{1}{4}$ pounds. The other weighs $4\frac{5}{8}$ pounds. What is the total weight?

   F $7\frac{1}{2}$ lb   **H** $8\frac{1}{4}$ lb

   G $7\frac{7}{8}$ lb   **I** $8\frac{1}{2}$ lb

3. A jug holds $3\frac{3}{8}$ quarts of juice. Hope pours out $1\frac{1}{8}$ quarts of juice. How much juice is left in the jug?

   A $2\frac{1}{8}$ qt   **C** $2\frac{1}{2}$ qt

   B $2\frac{1}{4}$ qt   **D** $4\frac{1}{2}$ qt

4. A watering can holds $3\frac{5}{8}$ gallons of water. Kensey uses $\frac{1}{2}$ of the water. How many gallons does she use?

   F $4\frac{1}{8}$ gal   **H** $2\frac{1}{16}$ gal

   G $3\frac{1}{4}$ gal   **I** $1\frac{13}{16}$ gal

Explain and solve.

5. Which is greater, 25% of 8 or $\frac{3}{8}$ of 8?

6. Erin had $1\frac{2}{3}$ bags of soil. She used 25% of the soil to fill a planter. How much soil did she use?

7. A store makes a profit of 20% of the selling price on each sale. Suppose the store sells $75 worth of merchandise. What is its profit?

8. A truck and its load of gravel weigh a total of $4\frac{1}{2}$ tons. The gravel is 75% of the total weight. How many tons of gravel are in the truck?

Connections

Find the area. Use the formula for the area of a triangle: $A = \frac{1}{2} \cdot (b \cdot h)$.

1. Area: _____

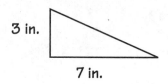

3 in.

7 in.

2. Area: _____

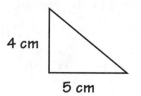

4 cm

5 cm

3. Area: _____

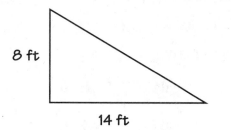

8 ft

14 ft

4. Area: _____

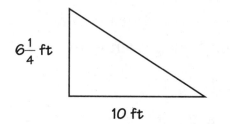

$6\frac{1}{4}$ ft

10 ft

5. Area: _____

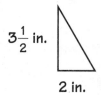

$3\frac{1}{2}$ in.

2 in.

6. Area: _____

3 yd

$4\frac{1}{8}$ yd

Find the volume. Use the formula $A = l \cdot w \cdot h$.

7. Volume: _____

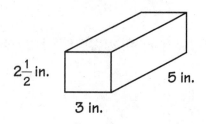

$2\frac{1}{2}$ in.

5 in.

3 in.

8. Volume: _____

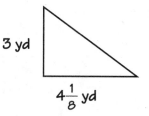

3 in.

6 in.

$4\frac{3}{4}$ in.

9. Volume: _____

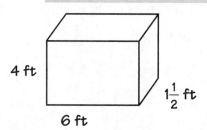

4 ft

$1\frac{1}{2}$ ft

6 ft

10. Volume: _____

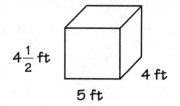

$4\frac{1}{2}$ ft

4 ft

5 ft

• TOPIC 6: Fractions, Mixed Numbers, and Percent Lesson 25

TOPIC 7

Probability and Statistics

Outcomes

REACHING MY GOAL
Determine how likely an event is by analyzing the possible outcomes.
(MA.E.2.2.2)
How did I do?

A. Each possible result of a probability experiment is an **outcome**.

When you roll the octahedron, you don't know which face will appear up. Each face represents an outcome.

The octahedron has 8 faces. So there are _____ possible outcomes.

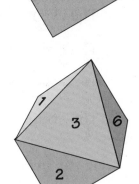

B. A named outcome or group of outcomes is called an **event**. An event that includes no possible outcomes is **impossible**. An event that includes at least one possible outcome is **possible**. An event that includes all possible outcomes is **certain**.

The octahedron's faces are labeled 1, 2, 3, 3, 4, 5, 6, and 6. How many outcomes are there for the event of rolling a 3?

_____

How many outcomes are there for the event of rolling a whole number? _____

So, the event of rolling a whole number is *certain*.

How many outcomes are there for the event of rolling a 7? _____

So, the event of rolling a 7 is _____ .

C. If one event includes more outcomes than another event, the first event is **more likely** than the second event. If two or more events have the same number of outcomes, they are **equally likely**.

Example 1

Use the labeled octahedron. **Which event is more likely, rolling a 2 or a 3?**

The event of rolling a 2 includes one outcome.

The event of rolling a 3 includes _____ outcomes.

So, rolling a _____ is more likely.

Example 2

On the labeled octahedron, suppose the 4 is changed to a 2. **Now which event is more likely, rolling a 2 or a 3?**

The event of rolling a 2 includes _____ outcomes.

The event of rolling a 3 includes _____ outcomes.

So, rolling a 2 or a 3 is _____ likely now.

Practice

Use the set of marbles to solve problems 1–8. Imagine picking a marble from a sack without looking.

Write *certain, possible,* or *impossible.*

1. The event of picking a green marble is _____ .

2. The event of picking a gray marble is _____ .

3. The event of picking a red marble is _____ .

4. The event of picking a marble that is *not* blue is _____ .

Circle the event that is *more* likely.

5. Picking a gray marble   Picking a white marble

6. Picking a gray marble   Picking a red marble

7. Picking a yellow marble   Picking a white marble

8. Picking a red marble   Picking a white marble

Use the set of fruits to solve the problems. Imagine picking a fruit from the set without looking.

9. Which kinds of fruit are equally likely to be picked?
_____

10. If a pear were replaced with a pineapple, which would be more likely, picking a pineapple or picking a banana? _____

11. In the original set, if a banana were replaced with an apple, which would be more likely, picking a pear or picking a banana?
_____

Problem Solving

1. Use the clues to find the numbers on the faces not shown.

   Clues

   - There are four different numbers you can roll.
   - The chance of rolling a number less than 6 is certain.
   - Rolling an even number is more likely than rolling an odd number.
   - The chance of rolling a 2 is the same as the chance of rolling a 4.

   The other faces are numbered ▢ , ▢ , and ▢ .

   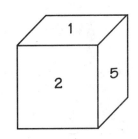

2. Use the clues to find the numbers of the other sectors.

   Clues

   - Spinning an odd number is impossible.
   - Spinning a number less than 14 is certain.
   - The chance of spinning a multiple of 3 is the same as the chance of spinning a multiple of 5.
   - Two outcomes are multiples of 4.

3. Use the clues to find the colors of the other marbles.

   Clues

   - There are four different colors you can pick.
   - Picking a green marble is the most likely.
   - Picking a red marble is the least likely.
   - G = Green, B = Blue, Y = Yellow, R = Red

4. Use the clues to find the numbers on the faces not shown.

   Clues

   - There are five different numbers you can roll.
   - Rolling a 2 is more likely than rolling a 5.
   - The chance of rolling a 3 is the same as the chance of rolling a 4.
   - The sum of all the outcomes is less than 20.

   The other faces are numbered ▢ , ▢ , ▢ , ▢ , and ▢ .

   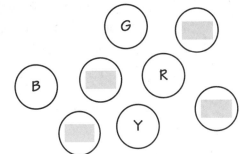

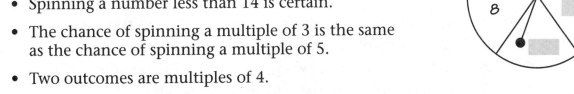

When you look at a clock, is the second hand more likely to be between the 11 and the 2 or between the 6 and the 8?

Connections

Write the missing fraction or decimal.

1. $\frac{1}{4} + \frac{3}{8} + $ ___ $ = 1$

2. $0.3 + 0.35 + $ ___ $ = 1$

3. $0.5 + $ ___ $ + 0.45 = 1$

4. $\frac{3}{5} + \frac{3}{10} + $ ___ $ = 1$

5. ___ $ + \frac{1}{6} + \frac{2}{3} = 1$

6. $0.25 + $ ___ $ + 0.55 = 1$

7. $1 - $ ___ $ - \frac{1}{4} = \frac{9}{16}$

8. $1 - $ ___ $ - 0.3 = 0.1$

9. $1 - 0.15 - $ ___ $ = 0.5$

10. $1 - \frac{3}{4} - $ ___ $ = \frac{1}{8}$

11. $1 - $ ___ $ - \frac{1}{5} = \frac{3}{10}$

12. $1 - 0.6 - $ ___ $ = 0.15$

Solve.

13. **a.** A bowling team bought pizza. Three more people ordered mushroom pizza than ordered anchovy pizza. One more person ordered anchovy pizza than ordered pepperoni pizza. Two people ordered pepperoni pizza. What fraction of the bowling team ordered anchovy pizza? ___

   b. The next week, one member of the team didn't go to the bowling alley. Of the people who did go, 3 had red bowling balls, 1 had a purple bowling ball, 2 had gold bowling balls, and the rest had black bowling balls. What percent of the bowlers had black bowling balls? ___

   c. The following week, the entire bowling team showed up. Also, 9 new members joined. What decimal part of the team are new members? ___

14. On Monday, Marge ate one piece of fruit. On Tuesday, she ate two pieces of fruit; on Wednesday, three pieces; and so on. She continued this pattern through Sunday. What fraction of the week's fruit did she eat on Sunday? ___

15. On Monday, Hank ate 9 vegetables. On Tuesday, he ate 7 vegetables; on Wednesday, 5 vegetables; and so on. He continued this pattern through Friday. Of all the vegetables he ate, what percent did he eat on Friday? ___

Experiments

REACHING MY GOAL
Conduct probability experiments and use the results to make statements about the experiments. (MA.E.2.2.1)

How did I do?

Each step of a **probability experiment** is conducted randomly, so the results are based on chance. You can use the results to draw conclusions about the items in the experiment.

A. Work with a partner to conduct the experiments.

Experiment 1

Put 1 red tile and 3 green tiles in a sack. Without looking, pick a tile from the sack. Mark the outcome—the color of the tile—on the tally chart. Return the tile to the sack. Do this until you have 8 outcomes.

Red Tiles	Green Tiles

What fraction of your outcomes are red?

What fraction of your outcomes are green?

Experiment 2

Replace one of the green tiles with a red tile. Repeat the steps of Experiment 1.

Red Tiles	Green Tiles

What fraction of your outcomes are red?

What fraction of your outcomes are green?

B. Share your results from the experiments with three or four other pairs of students. Add the outcomes.

What fraction of the total outcomes for Experiment 1 are red?

What fraction of the total outcomes for Experiment 1 are green?

What fraction of the total outcomes for Experiment 2 are red?

What fraction of the total outcomes for Experiment 2 are green?

Now use your results to draw some conclusions.

What do the red outcomes show when $\frac{1}{4}$ of the tiles are red?

What do the red outcomes show when $\frac{1}{2}$ of the tiles are red?

How did increasing the number of outcomes affect the fractions?

Practice

Work with a partner to conduct the experiment.

1. Toss a coin so that it lands on a flat surface. Mark the outcome—heads or tails—on the tally chart. Toss the coin until you have 10 outcomes.

Heads	Tails

   What fraction of the outcomes are heads? ▮▮▮▮
   What fraction of the outcomes are tails? ▮▮▮▮

2. Share your results from the experiment in problem 1 with three or four other pairs of students. Add the outcomes.

   What fraction of the total outcomes are heads? ▮▮▮
   What fraction of the total outcomes are tails? ▮▮▮
   How did increasing the number of outcomes affect the fractions? ▮▮▮

3. Toss a coin and make a mental note of the outcome. Try to predict the outcome of the *next* toss. Toss the coin again, and mark the outcome on the appropriate tally chart. Continue until you have 20 outcomes altogether. Share your results with two other pairs of students. Add the outcomes.

   After a Heads Toss

Heads	Tails

   After a Tails Toss

Heads	Tails

   After a heads toss, is the next outcome more likely to be a tails? ▮▮▮
   After a tails toss, is the next outcome more likely to be a heads? ▮▮▮

4. Now you can make a statement. Write *does* or *doesn't*.

   > In this probability experiment, one outcome ▮▮▮▮▮ affect another outcome.

5. Start with 5 green tiles and 5 red tiles. Don't look while your partner puts 6 of the tiles in a sack. Pick a tile from the sack, mark the outcome on the chart, and return the tile to the sack. Do this until you have 20 outcomes.

Red Tiles	Green Tiles

   Guess how many green tiles are in the sack. ▮▮▮
   Was your guess right? Explain how you made your guess.
   ▮▮▮▮▮▮▮▮▮▮

6. Repeat the experiment in problem 5, switching roles with your partner.

Problem Solving

In a fair game, each player has the same chance of winning. **Play each game with a partner, and then answer the questions.**

Two-Coin Louie

Rules

- A player tosses two coins at once.
- Players take turns tossing the coins.
- Mark the outcomes on the chart.
- One player gets a point for a toss of heads-tails.
- The other player gets a point for a toss of tails-tails or a toss of heads-heads.
- The first player to get 10 points wins.

Heads-Tails   Tails-Tails   Heads-Heads

1. What fraction of your outcomes were heads-tails?

2. What fraction of your outcomes were tails-tails?

3. What fraction of your outcomes were heads-heads?

4. Is Two-Coin Louie a fair game?

Three-Coin Bella

Rules

- A player tosses three coins at once.
- Players take turns tossing the coins.
- Mark the outcomes on the chart.
- One player gets a point for a "mixed" toss, such as heads-tails-heads or tails-tails-heads.
- The other player gets a point for a "straight" toss of tails-tails-tails or heads-heads-heads.
- The first player to get 10 points wins.

Mixed Tosses   Straight Tosses

5. What fraction of your outcomes were mixed tosses?

6. What fraction of your outcomes were straight tosses?

7. Is Three-Coin Bella a fair game?

Invent a new fair game with three coins. Explain how the points are scored.

Connections

Answer the questions about each tally chart.

1. <u>Blue Marbles</u>   <u>Orange Marbles</u>
   卌 ||| 卌 卌 ||

   What percent of the marbles are blue?

   What percent of the marbles are not blue?

2. <u>Romances</u>   <u>Mysteries</u>
   卌 卌 卌 | 卌 ||||

   What fraction of the books are romances?
   What percent of the books are mysteries?

3. <u>Dimes</u>   <u>Pennies</u>
   ||| 卌 ||

   What percent of the coins are pennies?

   What percent of the coins are not pennies?

4. <u>Yellow Tiles</u>   <u>Blue Tiles</u>   <u>Red Tiles</u>
   卌 || 卌 |||| ||||

   What fraction of the tiles are red?

   What percent of the tiles are not red?

5. <u>Tetras</u>   <u>Angelfish</u>   <u>Swordtails</u>
   卌 卌   卌 || 卌 卌 |

   What percent of the fish are angelfish?

   What fraction of the fish are tetras?

6. <u>Almonds</u>   <u>Walnuts</u>   <u>Pecans</u>
   ||| 卌 | 卌 ||||

   What fraction of the nuts are almonds?

   What percent of the nuts are not pecans?

7. <u>Vowels</u>   <u>Consonants</u>
   卌 卌 || 卌 卌 卌 卌 ||||

   What fraction of the letters are vowels?

   What fraction of the letters are not vowels?

8. <u>Swimmers</u>   <u>Cyclists</u>
   卌 卌 ||| 卌 ||

   What percent of the people are swimmers?
   What percent of the people are cyclists?

ALGEBRA READINESS

Compare. Write <, >, or =.

9. $\frac{12}{20}$ 0.6

10. 50% $\frac{11}{25}$

11. $\frac{3}{8}$ $\frac{10}{32}$

12. 0.75 $\frac{20}{24}$

13. $\frac{2}{5}$ 30%

14. $\frac{18}{36}$ $\frac{13}{26}$

Probability

REACHING MY GOAL
Determine the likelihood of an outcome, and express a probability as a fraction. (MA.E.2.2.2)

How did I do? ✓✓✓

You can use a number to describe probability.

- If an outcome is **impossible**, its probability is **0**.

- If an outcome is **certain**, its probability is **1**.

- The probability of a **possible** outcome can be stated as a fraction, a decimal, or a percent that is greater than 0 but not greater than 1.

Example 1

A game can be played with the game board at the right by tossing tokens onto the board.

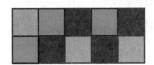

What is the probability of landing on a green square?

The board has no green squares. Landing on green is impossible. So, the probability of landing on a green square is 0.

Example 2

What is the probability of landing on red or gray or black?

All the squares are red, gray, or black. Landing on one of the squares is certain. So, the probability of landing on red or gray or black is 1.

Example 3

What is the probability of landing on a red square?

a. There are 10 possible outcomes. Landing on a red square is a positive outcome. The board has 3 red squares. So, there is a 3 in 10 chance of landing on red.

Write the probability as the positive outcomes over the possible outcomes. $\dfrac{3}{10}$ ← positive outcomes ← possible outcomes

So, the probability of landing on a red square is $\dfrac{3}{}$.

b. The probability $\dfrac{3}{10}$ can be written as a decimal, 0.3, or as a percent, 30%.

Example 4

What is the probability of landing on black?

There are 10 possible outcomes. Landing on black is a positive outcome. The board has 4 black squares. So, there is a _____ in _____ chance of landing on black.

The probability of landing on black is $\dfrac{4}{10}$, or $\dfrac{}{5}$. This probability stated as a decimal or a percent is 0.4 or _____%.

Practice

When the probability of an event is greater than $\frac{1}{2}$, the event is **likely**.

When the probability of an event is less than $\frac{1}{2}$, the event is **unlikely**.

When two or more events have the same probability, the events are **equally likely**.

1. Suppose you pick a marble from the bag at the right.
   Which two events are equally likely?

   Find the two events that have the same probability.

   The probability of picking black is $\frac{2}{12}$.

   The probability of picking ▢▢ is $\frac{2}{12}$.

   So, picking ▢▢ and picking ▢▢ are equally likely events.

2. Suppose you pick a marble from the bag. Which event is likely?

   Find the event that has a probability greater than $\frac{1}{2}$.

   The probability of picking ▢▢ is $\frac{7}{12}$.

   So, picking ▢▢ is a likely event.

3. Is picking a gray marble or a pink marble likely or unlikely?

   Find the probability of picking gray or pink.

   $\dfrac{\text{positive outcomes} \rightarrow}{\text{possible outcomes} \rightarrow}$ $\dfrac{\text{gray marbles + pink marble} \rightarrow}{\text{total marbles} \rightarrow}$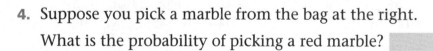

   So, picking gray or pink is ▢▢▢ .

4. Suppose you pick a marble from the bag at the right.
   What is the probability of picking a red marble? ▢▢

5. Suppose you pick a marble from the bag at the right.
   What is the probability of picking a marble that is not red? ▢▢

6. Suppose you pick a marble from the bag at the right.
   What is the probability of picking a gray marble or a red marble? ▢▢

7. Suppose you pick a marble from the bag at the right.
   Is picking a black marble or a gray marble a likely or an unlikely event? ▢▢

8. Suppose you pick a marble from the bag at the right.
   Which two events are equally likely?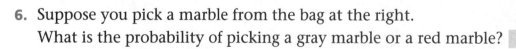

• TOPIC 7: Probability and Statistics Lesson 3

Problem Solving

Use the clues to solve the problems.

The coins used in each set are pennies, nickels, dimes, and quarters.

1. Two coins are removed from the set shown at the right, and then a coin is picked at random.

   • Picking a quarter and picking a penny are equally likely.

   • The probability of picking a dime is 0.

   Which two coins are removed from the set? ▨▨▨▨▨

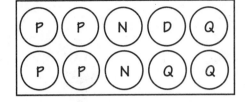

2. One coin is added to the set shown at the right, and then a coin is picked at random.

   • Picking a quarter and picking a penny are equally likely.

   • Picking a nickel is more likely than picking a dime.

   Which coin is added to the set? ▨▨▨▨▨

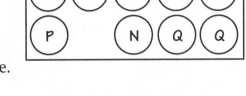

3. Three coins are added to the set shown at the right, and then a coin is picked at random.

   • Picking a nickel and picking a penny are equally likely.

   • The probability of picking a dime is $\frac{1}{4}$.

   Which three coins are added to the set? ▨▨▨▨▨

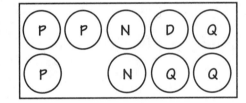

4. Three coins are removed from the set shown at the right, and then a coin is picked at random.

   • Picking a quarter and picking a penny are equally likely.

   • Picking a nickel is not more likely than picking a dime.

   Which three coins are removed from the set?

   ▨▨▨▨▨

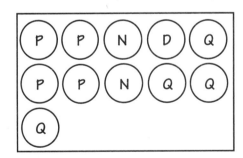

5. A coin is picked at random from a set of 8 coins.

   • Picking a dime is a likely event.

   • Picking a nickel is more likely than picking a penny.

   Write the number of each kind of coin in the set: pennies ▨▨▨ , nickels ▨▨▨ , dimes ▨▨▨ , quarters ▨▨▨ .

Connections

Use the graph to solve problems 1–5.

1. How many birds in all did John see last year?

2. What percent of the total number of birds did John see in the spring?

3. What percent of the total number of birds did John see in the summer?

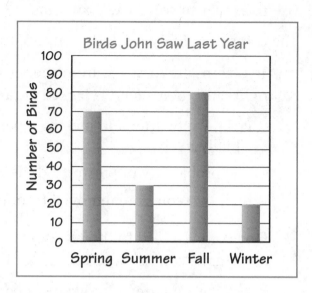

4. What fraction of the total number of birds did John see in the winter?

5. In which season is John most likely to see a bird?

   In which season is John least likely to see a bird?

ALGEBRA READINESS

Find the missing addend.

6. $\frac{3}{16} +$ ___ $= 1$

7. $0.65 +$ ___ $= 1$

8. $\frac{7}{12} +$ ___ $= 1$

9. $0.45 +$ ___ $= 1$

Compare. Write <, >, or =.

10. $\frac{4}{5}$ ⬭ 0.70

11. 60% ⬭ $\frac{13}{20}$

12. 0.25 ⬭ $\frac{3}{10}$

13. $\frac{4}{5}$ ⬭ 80%

LANGUAGE OF MATHEMATICS

Use a word from the box to complete the sentence.

| unlikely | likely |
| impossible | certain |

14. An event that is ___ has a probability of greater than 50%.

15. An event that is ___ has a probability of 100%.

16. An event that is ___ has a probability of less than 0.5.

17. An event that is ___ has a probability of 0.

Making Inferences from Outcomes

REACHING MY GOAL
Use the outcomes of experiments
to make inferences. (MA.E.2.2.2)

How did I do?

In an experiment such as drawing from a set of marbles, the outcomes of the experiment allow you to make inferences or predictions about the contents of the set.

Example 1

Marble	Times Drawn
Blue	6
Green	10
Red	4

A marble is drawn 20 times from a bag containing 10 marbles. The marble is returned to the bag each time. The table shows the results of the draws. **How many blue marbles are likely to be in the bag?**

The fraction of drawn marbles that are blue and the fraction of marbles in the bag that are blue are likely to be about the same.

> **THINK**
> There are at least 3 colors of marbles. There might be more.

Solve for the equivalent fraction.

blue marbles drawn → $\dfrac{6}{20}$ = $\dfrac{?}{10}$ ← blue marbles in bag
total marbles drawn →   ← total marbles in bag

$\dfrac{6}{20} = \dfrac{}{10}$

It is likely that there are about ▢ blue marbles in the bag.

Example 2

Marble	Times Drawn
Black	1
Blue	10
Green	6
Red	3

The experiment is repeated. The table shows the results of the draws. **Add the results of the two experiments, then revise your prediction about the number of blue marbles.**

blue marbles drawn → $\dfrac{6 + 10}{20 + 20}$ = $\dfrac{?}{10}$ ← blue marbles in bag
total marbles drawn →   ← total marbles in bag

Solve for the equivalent fraction.

$\dfrac{16}{40} = \dfrac{}{10}$

Now it seems likely that there are about ▢ blue marbles in the bag.

Example 3

Marble	Number
Black	1
Blue	5
Green	3
Red	1

The table shows the actual contents of the bag. **Was either of your inferences about the number of blue marbles correct?** ▢

Was your second inference more accurate? ▢
Doing more experiments usually makes your inferences more accurate, but they still may not be correct.

Practice

1. A marble is drawn 60 times from a bag containing 10 marbles. The marble is returned to the bag each time. The table shows the results of the draws. How many more red marbles than blue marbles are likely to be in the bag?

Marble	Times Drawn
Blue	12
Green	6
Red	24
Yellow	18

   a. Set up and solve equivalent fractions to predict how many red marbles are in the bag.

   red marbles drawn $\longrightarrow$ $\dfrac{24}{60} = \dfrac{?}{10}$ $\longleftarrow$ red marbles in bag
   total marbles drawn $\longrightarrow$ $\phantom{\dfrac{24}{60}}$ $\longleftarrow$ total marbles in bag

   $\dfrac{24}{60} = \dfrac{}{10}$ There are likely to be _____ red marbles in the bag.

   b. Set up and solve equivalent fractions to predict how many blue marbles are in the bag.

   blue marbles drawn $\longrightarrow$ $\dfrac{12}{60} = \dfrac{?}{10}$ $\longleftarrow$ blue marbles in bag
   total marbles drawn $\longrightarrow$ $\phantom{\dfrac{12}{60}}$ $\longleftarrow$ total marbles in bag

   $\dfrac{12}{60} = \dfrac{}{10}$ There are likely to be _____ blue marbles in the bag.

   c. Find the difference between your predictions.

   So, it is likely that there are about _____ more red marbles than blue marbles in the bag.

Use the information and the table to solve the problem. Circle the letter of the correct answer.

A marble is drawn 80 times from a bag containing 20 marbles. The marble is returned to the bag each time. The table shows the results of the draws.

Marble	Times Drawn
Black	16
Blue	20
Purple	24
White	20

2. How many purple marbles are likely to be in the bag?

   F 3   **H** 5

   G 4   **I** 6

3. How many white marbles are likely to be in the bag?

   A 3   **C** 5

   B 4   **D** 6

4. It is _____ that there are more purple marbles than black marbles in the bag.

   F certain   **H** unlikely

   G likely   **I** impossible

5. It is _____ that there are brown marbles in the bag.

   A certain   **C** possible

   B likely   **D** impossible

Problem Solving

Manny's Matching Marble Game

- Play with a partner.

- Player A places 10 marbles of 3 colors in a bag. No two colors can have the same number of marbles. Player B should not see which marbles went in the bag.

- Player B draws a marble from the bag 20 times. The marble is returned to the bag each time.

- Using the outcomes of the draws, Player B predicts what the contents of the bag are.

- Player B then asks Player A to replace a marble of one color with a marble of another color. Player B names the two colors. The goal is to have two colors of marbles with the same number of marbles. This is called a match.

- If Player B makes a match, he or she gets 1 point.

- Player B should then pick 10 marbles and have Player A try to create a match.

- The player with the most points at the end of play wins the game.

Example

The outcomes of 20 draws are shown in the table. You may predict that the contents of the bag are 5 black marbles, 4 red marbles, and 1 pink marble. That gives you two choices:

Marble	Times Drawn
Black	11
Pink	2
Red	7

- replace a black marble with a pink one, leaving 4 black, 4 red, and 2 pink marbles;

- replace the pink marble with a red one, leaving 5 black and 5 red marbles.

You can copy these tables for your games.

Marble	Times Drawn

Marble	Times Drawn

Do you think you would get a better score if you picked 40 marbles each time? Try it!

Connections

1. A marble was drawn 60 times from a bag. The graph shows the fraction of total draws represented by each color. Complete the table.

Marble	Times Drawn
Black	
Gray	
Red	
White	

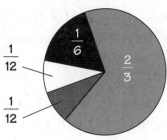

2. A marble was drawn 60 times from a bag. The graph shows the fraction of total draws represented by each color. Complete the table.

Marble	Times Drawn
Black	
Gray	
Pink	
Red	
White	

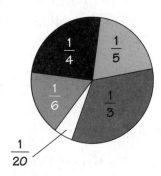

3. A marble was drawn 50 times from a bag. The graph shows the percent of total draws represented by each color. Complete the table.

Marble	Times Drawn
Black	
Gray	
Pink	
Red	
White	

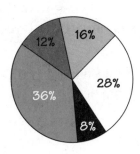

ALGEBRA READINESS

Solve for the equivalent fraction.

4. $\dfrac{2}{3} = \dfrac{\boxed{}}{18}$

5. $\dfrac{3}{8} = \dfrac{9}{\boxed{}}$

6. $\dfrac{9}{45} = \dfrac{1}{\boxed{}}$

7. $\dfrac{49}{56} = \dfrac{\boxed{}}{8}$

8. $\dfrac{4}{5} = \dfrac{\boxed{}}{30}$

9. $\dfrac{8}{15} = \dfrac{32}{\boxed{}}$

Spinner Predictions

REACHING MY GOAL
Use spinners to identify the possible outcomes of an experiment. (MA.E.2.2.2)

How did I do?

The different sections of a spinner are called **sectors**. The larger a sector, the more likely it is that the pointer will land on that sector.

In the spinner at the right, sector C is larger than sector F. So, the pointer is more likely to land on C than on F.

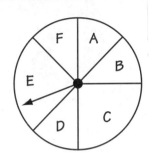

A. The probability that the pointer will land on a sector of the spinner is equal to the fraction of the spinner covered by the sector.

Example 1

Sector A covers $\frac{1}{8}$ of the spinner and sector C covers $\frac{1}{4}$ of the spinner. **What is the probability that the pointer will land on sector E?**

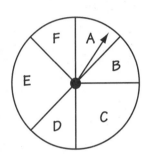

Find the fraction of the spinner covered by sector E. It is the same fraction as sector C, or $\frac{1}{4}$ of the spinner.

So, the probability that the pointer will land on sector E is ▭ .

B. You can use probability to predict how many times the pointer is likely to land on a sector in a given number of spins.

Example 2

Each of the gray and red sectors covers $\frac{1}{4}$ of the spinner, and the black and the white sectors each cover $\frac{1}{8}$ of the spinner. **How many times is the pointer likely to land on red if you spin 40 times? How many times is it likely to land on white?**

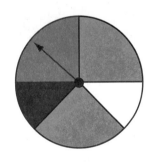

Step 1: Find the probability of getting each color with one spin.

Red   =   2 × ▭   →   ▭

White   =   ▭

Step 2: Multiply the probability for each color by the number of spins.

Red   =   40 × ▭   →   ▭

White   =   40 × ▭   →   ▭

So, with 40 spins, it is likely that the pointer will land on red about ▭ times and on white about ▭ times.

Practice

Use spinners A and B to solve problems 1–4.

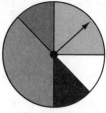

Spinner A

Spinner B

1. Is the pointer more likely to land on red on spinner A or on spinner B?

2. What is the probability of the pointer landing on gray on spinner B?

3. Name one color that is equally likely on spinner A and on spinner B.

4. Predict how many times the pointer will land on each color if spinner A is spun 80 times.

   black _____   gray _____   pink _____
   red _____   white _____

Use the spinner at the right to solve problems 5–7.

5. Estimate the probability in tenths that the pointer will land on each color. Write your answer as a fraction.

   black _____   gray _____
   red _____   white _____

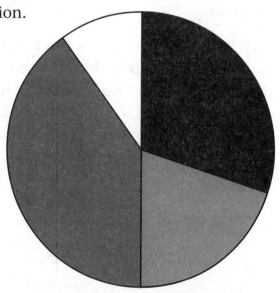

6. Predict how many times the pointer will land on each color if the spinner is spun 30 times. Be sure that your predictions add up to 30.

   black _____   gray _____
   red _____   white _____

7. Use a pencil and a paper clip on the spinner to test your predictions. Write your results for 30 spins.

   black _____   gray _____
   red _____   white _____

Hint: $\frac{1}{2}$ of the spinner $= \frac{5}{10}$.

• TOPIC 7: Probability and Statistics Lesson 5

Problem Solving

Use the picture and the information below to solve the problems on this page.

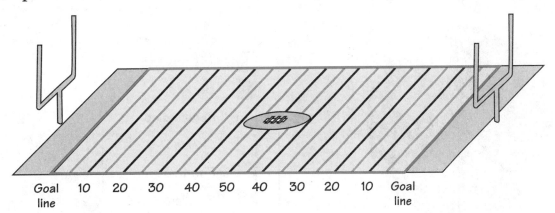

| Goal line | 10 | 20 | 30 | 40 | 50 | 40 | 30 | 20 | 10 | Goal line |

Morty lost his lucky silver dollar on the football field. He and his four brothers each took a part of the field to search for the silver dollar. One of the brothers found the coin.

Name	Part of Field
Morty	the goal line to the 25 yard line
Jake	the 25 yard line to the 40 yard line
Dylan	the 40 yard line to the 50 yard line
Elliot	the 50 yard line to the 30 yard line
Joel	the 30 yard line to the goal line

Circle the letter of the correct answer.

1. What is the probability that Morty found the silver dollar?

   A 0.25% **C** 25%

   B 0.4% **D** 40%

2. What is the probability that Joel found the silver dollar?

   F 30% **H** 70%

   G 50% **I** 100%

3. What is the probability that Elliot found the silver dollar?

   A 20% **C** 50%

   B 30% **D** 70%

4. What is the probability that one of the brothers found the silver dollar?

   F 5% **H** 50%

   G 20% **I** 100%

Morty and his brothers found many other coins when they searched the football field. The types of coins they found are shown in the table at the right.

5. Predict how many quarters Morty found.

6. Predict how many pennies Jake found.

7. Predict how many dimes Dylan found.

8. Predict how many nickels Elliot found.

Coin	Number Found
Penny	60
Nickel	45
Dime	40
Quarter	16

Connections

Use the spinner below to solve problems 1–5.

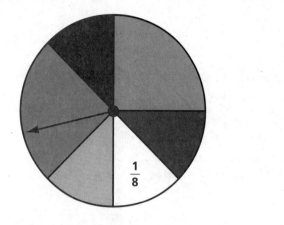

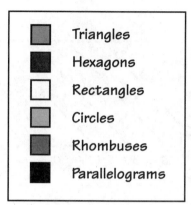

1. Find the probability of getting a quadrilateral.

2. Find the probability of getting a polygon.

3. Find the probability of getting a figure with 4 or more sides.

4. Find the probability of getting a figure that has diagonals.

5. Find the probability of getting a figure the sum of whose angles is 180°.

Use the stem-and-leaf plot at the right to solve problems 6–9.

6. Find the range of ages of people at the reunion.

7. How many people at the reunion are over the age of 40?

8. There is a prize hidden in the cake at the reunion. Every person gets one slice of cake. Find the probability that Shirley, the oldest person, will get the prize.

9. Find the probability that a person who is 20 or younger will get the prize.

Ages of People at Thompson Family Reunion

Stem	Leaf				
0	6	2	8	8	
1	6	1	2	6	9
2	2	0	9	4	
3	3	6	7		
4	5	8	6		
5					
6					
7	1				

What is the probability that a square is also a rhombus?

Using Graphs to Find Probability

REACHING MY GOAL
Use data in graphs to find the probability of an event. (MA.E.2.2.1)

How did I do?

A. You can use the data in graphs to find the probability of an event.

Example 1

Craig Biggio got a hit in his first at-bat in a game. Find the probability that it was a home run.

> **THINK**
> The positive outcomes are the number of home runs. The possible outcomes are the total of all types of hits.

Craig Biggio's Hits by Type (2001)

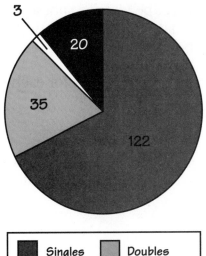

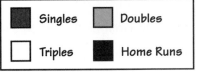

Step 1: Add the totals for each type of hit to find Biggio's total hits for the year.

$122 + 35 + 3 + 20 = $

Step 2: Find the fraction of Biggio's total hits that home runs represent.

$\frac{20}{180} = $

So, the probability that Biggio hit a home run is   .

B. You can use probability to predict future events.

Example 2

Of Craig Biggio's next 45 hits, how many are likely to be home runs?

> **THINK**
> I can find the positive outcomes by multiplying the probability by the possible outcomes. The possible outcomes are the 45 hits.

Multiply the probability that Biggio will hit a home run by the number of additional hits.

$\frac{1}{9} \times 45 = $

So, of Biggio's next 45 hits,   are likely to be home runs.

Practice

Felipe began bird-watching one year ago. Matty has been bird-watching for six months. The graph shows the total number of birds, by type, that Felipe and Matty have spotted.

Use the graph to solve the problems on this page.

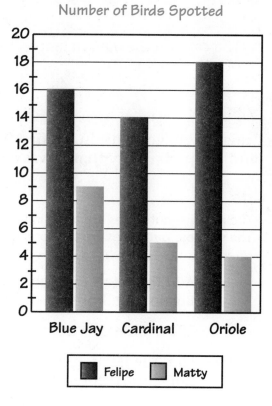

Number of Birds Spotted

Blue Jay   Cardinal   Oriole

■ Felipe   □ Matty

1. If Felipe were to spot a bird tomorrow, what is the probability that it would be a blue jay?

   a. Add the totals for each type of bird Felipe spotted.

   [ ] + [ ] + [ ] = [ ]

   b. Find the fraction of all the birds Felipe spotted that blue jays represent.

   [ ]
   ―― = [ ]
   [ ]

   So, the probability that Felipe will spot a blue jay is [ ].

2. If Felipe and Matty each spot a bird, is Felipe more likely or less likely than Matty to spot a blue jay?

   a. Add the totals for each type of bird Matty spotted.

   [ ] + [ ] + [ ] = [ ]

   b. Find the fraction of all the birds Matty spotted that blue jays represent.

   [ ]
   ―― = [ ]
   [ ]

   c. Compare the probability that Felipe will spot a blue jay to the probability that Matty will spot one. Write <, >, or =.

   $\frac{1}{3}$ ⬭ $\frac{1}{2}$

   So, Felipe is [ ] likely to spot a blue jay than Matty is.

> **THINK**
> The greater the fraction, the higher the probability that an event will occur.

Problem Solving

Use the graphs to solve the problems on this page.

Lunch Served at Spellman School

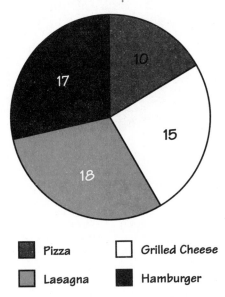

Lunch Served at Fremont School

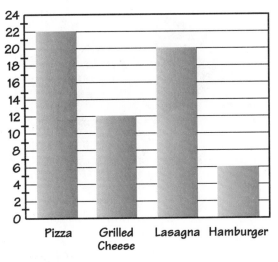

- ■ Pizza
- □ Grilled Cheese
- ■ Lasagna
- ■ Hamburger

Circle the letter of the correct answer.

1. What is the probability that a student at Spellman School will have pizza for lunch?

   A $\frac{1}{60}$ **C** $\frac{1}{6}$

   B $\frac{1}{10}$ **D** $\frac{1}{5}$

2. What is the probability that a student at Fremont School will have a hamburger for lunch?

   F 6%   **H** 16%

   G 10%   **I** 20%

3. In her next 30 lunches, how many times is a Fremont student likely to have lasagna?

   A 10   **C** 15

   B 12   **D** 20

4. How many times would a Spellman student have to eat lunch to be likely to have lasagna 6 times?

   F 10   **H** 20

   G 18   **I** 24

5. Out of 48 lunches, how many more times is a Spellman student likely to have grilled cheese than pizza?

   A 4   **C** 8

   B 5   **D** 12

6. How many more lunches than a Spellman student would a Fremont student have to eat so that each student probably had grilled cheese 20 times?

   F 20   **H** 80

   G 25   **I** 100

> Can the probability of an event ever be written as a mixed number?

Connections

Use the graph to solve problems 1–5. Write your answers in simplest form.

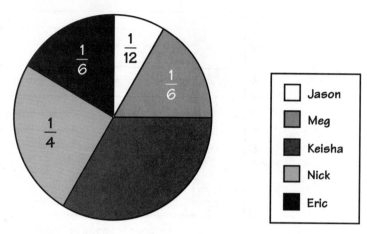

Cars Washed Last Summer

1. What fraction of the cars did Keisha wash?

2. If a total of 240 cars were washed, how many did Eric wash?

3. How many more cars did Nick wash than Jason washed?

4. Find the probability that a car from the set of 240 cars was *not* washed by Meg.

5. If 120 more cars were washed, how many of those cars would Keisha and Nick together be likely to wash?

Find the product. Write your answer in simplest form.

6. $\frac{3}{4} \times 28 =$

7. $\frac{1}{6} \times 14 =$

8. $15 \times \frac{4}{9} =$

9. $20 \times \frac{3}{8} =$

10. $\frac{2}{5} \times 16 =$

11. $\frac{3}{7} \times 35 =$

12. $21 \times \frac{5}{6} =$

13. $17 \times \frac{3}{10} =$

ALGEBRA READINESS

Compare. Write <, >, or =.

14. $\frac{2}{3}$ ⬭ $\frac{5}{9}$

15. $\frac{3}{8}$ ⬭ $\frac{4}{7}$

16. $\frac{3}{4} \times 4$ ⬭ $\frac{1}{3} \times 9$

17. $\frac{5}{9} \times 7$ ⬭ $\frac{4}{9} \times 8$

Listing and Counting Possible Outcomes

REACHING MY GOAL
List and count to determine all possible outcomes for an event. (MA.E.2.2.1)

How did I do?

A. Outcomes that have more than one event can be shown with a tree diagram or an organized list.

Example 1

A store selling ice-cream cones offers 2 kinds of cones and 3 flavors of ice cream. **How many choices of cone and ice-cream flavor can be made?**

Make a tree diagram or an organized list to show all possible outcomes. Use letters to stand for the different cones and ice-cream flavors.

Tree Diagram

Cone	Ice-Cream Flavor	Cone and Flavor
Waffle Cone (W)	Chocolate (C)	WC
	Vanilla (V)	WV
	Strawberry (S)	WS
Flat Cone (F)	Chocolate (C)	FC
	Vanilla (V)	FV
	Strawberry (S)	FS

Organized List

	Choc	Van	Straw
Waffle (W)	WC	WV	WS
Flat (F)	FC	FV	FS

So, 6 choices of cone and flavor can be made.

Because there are 2 kinds of cones and 3 flavors, the number of outcomes is 2×3, or 6.

B. Sometimes, it is more important to list the possible outcomes of an event than to count them.

Example 2

Suppose you are choosing an ice-cream cone that has 2 scoops. Either scoop can be vanilla, chocolate, or strawberry. **How many different cones have vanilla? Complete the organized list.**

Count the outcomes that have vanilla.

There are _____ different cones that have vanilla.

Second Scoop

First Scoop	V	C	S
V	VV	VC	
C	CV	CC	CS
S	SV		SS

Practice

Complete the tree diagram to solve problems 1–3.

1. Two counters are blue on one side and red on the other. If you toss one after the other, how many outcomes are possible?

   Think: I can also multiply to find the number of outcomes.

   2 choices × 2 choices = 4

   So, [ ] outcomes are possible.

First Toss	Second Toss	Outcomes
Blue	Blue	BB
	Red	[ ]
Red	Blue	RB
	Red	[ ]

2. In how many outcomes will red be possible?

3. In how many outcomes will both counters be the same color?

Complete the organized list to solve problems 4–6.

4. How many 2-digit numbers formed with the digits *1*, *2*, and *3* are multiples of 11?

   [ ] 2-digit numbers

	1	2	3
1	11	12	13
2	21	[ ]	[ ]
3	[ ]	[ ]	[ ]

5. How many of the 2-digit numbers are even?

6. How many of the 2-digit numbers are less than 30?

Solve.

7. Jim has 5 shirts and 4 ties. How many combinations of shirts and ties can he make?

8. Bob has 4 shirts and 5 ties. How many combinations of shirts and ties can he make?

What do you notice about the last two problems on this page? Which property of multiplication do the two problems show?

Problem Solving

1. Pat has a pair of black pants and a pair of gray pants. She has a black shirt, a white shirt, and a gray shirt. She has a pair of black shoes and a pair of gray shoes. How many outfits can Pat make?

   Think: [　] pants × [　] shirts × [　] shoes = [　] combinations.

   Pat can make [　] outfits.

Complete the tree diagram to solve problems 2–4.

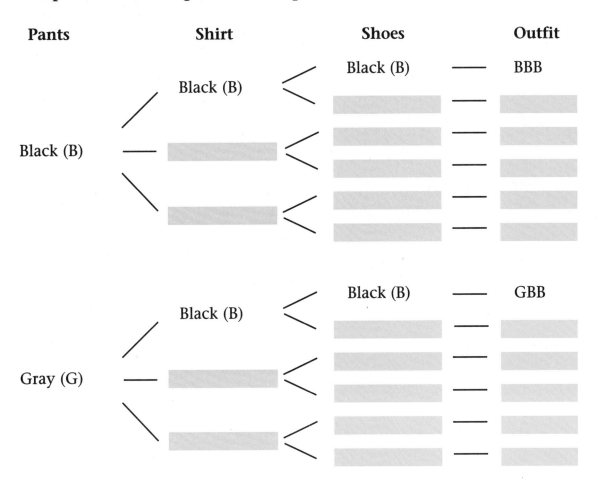

Pants	Shirt	Shoes	Outfit

2. How many of the outfits have gray shoes? [　]

3. How many of the outfits have a white shirt? [　]

4. How many of the outfits are all the same color? [　]

Connections

Solve.

1. A plant is making license plates. Each plate will have one of the numbers from 1 through 65 paired with one of the 26 letters of the alphabet. Each number will be paired once with each letter of the alphabet. How many different license plates can the plant make?

2. A mother has 35 choices for the first name of her new baby. She has 24 choices for the baby's middle name. How many different combinations of first name and middle name could she choose from to name her baby?

Find the prime factorization of the number.

3. 392

4. 110

5. 182

6. 85

7. 91

8. 210

ALGEBRA READINESS

Solve. You can use the prime factors you found in problems 3–8.

9. A cowboy store sells hats that have leather-and-silver hatbands. There are 91 different combinations possible. If there are 7 styles of hatbands, how many styles of hats are there?

10. An artist made a series of designs, each of which had a triangular shape and a curved shape. The artist used 17 triangular shapes and made 85 designs. How many curved shapes did the artist use?

11. A clothing designer came up with 182 two-piece outfits based on 7 kinds of pants. The other part of each outfit was a shirt. How many different shirts did the designer use?

12. Another designer came up with 110 two-piece outfits based on 5 kinds of skirts. The other part of each outfit was a blouse. How many different blouses did the designer use?

More About Probability

REACHING MY GOAL
Find the probability of a particular event from a set of all possible outcomes. (MA.E.2.2.1)

How did I do?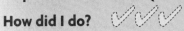

A. Tree diagrams can help to find probabilities.

Example

Matt has 3 pairs of socks: blue, white, and red. The socks are loose in a drawer. Suppose he were to dress in the dark, reaching into his sock drawer and taking 2 socks. **What is the probability of picking a matching pair of socks?**

Make a tree diagram to show all possible outcomes. Use letters and numbers to name the socks. For example, the blue pair would be named B1 and B2 for the 2 socks in the pair.

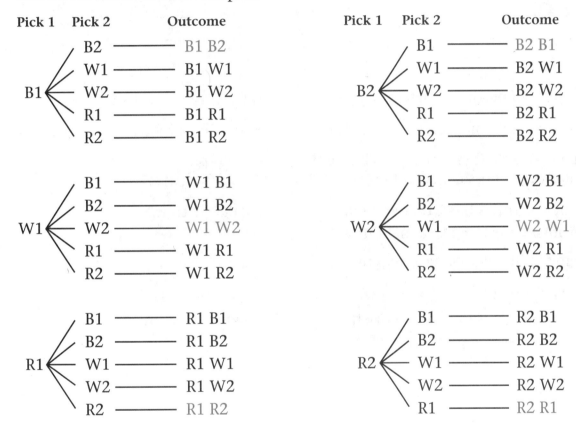

There are 30 possible outcomes but only 6 matching pairs.

So, the probability of picking a matching pair of socks is $\frac{6}{30}$, or $\frac{1}{5}$.

B. You can also use a mathematical method to find the probability of picking a matching pair of socks.

There are 6 possible outcomes for the first sock picked. After the first sock, there are 5 different second possibilities.

So, the number of possible outcomes is $6 \times 5 = 30$.

Each of the 6 socks has 1 that makes a pair with it. So, there are 6 ways to make a pair.

So, the probability is $\frac{6}{30}$, or $\frac{1}{5}$.

Practice

1. Marcia has 2 pairs of button earrings. The pairs are gold and silver. If she picks 2 earrings out of her jewelry box without looking, what is the probability of picking a matching pair? Complete the tree diagram to solve.

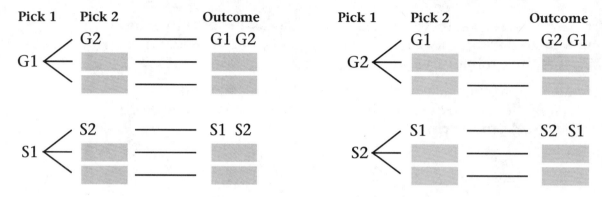

The probability of picking a matching pair is ⬚, or ⬚.

2. Complete the mathematical method that can be used to solve Problem 1.

   After each first pick, there are 3 possibilities for the second pick.
   So, the number of possible outcomes is $4 \times$ ⬚ $= 12$ outcomes.

   Each of the 4 earrings has 1 that will make a matching pair with it.
   So, there are 4 ways to make a matching pair. $\frac{4}{12} = \frac{1}{3}$

   So, the probability of picking a matching pair of earrings is ⬚.

3. Sam spins a spinner that is $\frac{1}{3}$ red, $\frac{1}{3}$ white, and $\frac{1}{3}$ gray. If Sam spins the spinner twice, what is the probability that he will spin gray both times? Complete the tree diagram to solve.

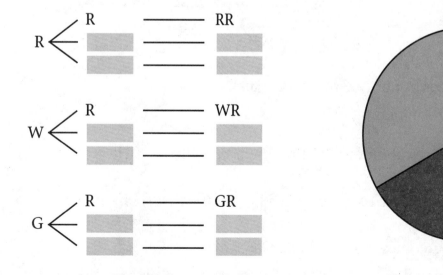

The probability that Sam will spin gray both times is ⬚.

Problem Solving

Complete the tree diagram to solve the problem.

1. Mike tosses a coin 4 times. What is the probability that he will toss tails, tails, heads, tails?

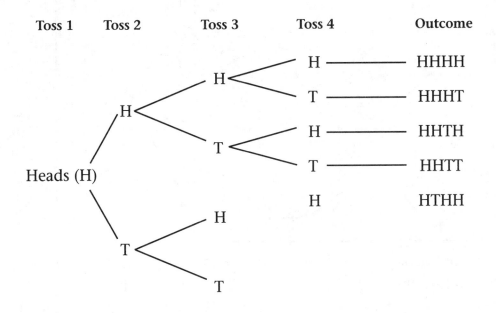

Toss 1	Toss 2	Toss 3	Toss 4	Outcome

Heads (H)

Tails (T)

The probability that he will toss tails, tails, heads, tails is ____.

Solve. Use a tree diagram if you wish.

2. John has brown slacks and gray slacks, a white shirt and a gray shirt, and a tan jacket and a gray jacket. What is the probability that he will wear an outfit with exactly 2 gray items in it next Tuesday? ____

3. Suez has carnations, roses, and tulips. She has 1 pink and 1 red carnation, 1 pink and 2 red roses, and 2 red tulips. If she takes 1 of each kind at random, what is the probability of having all 3 red? ____

Connections

Use the map to solve problems 1–6.

Map of Johnson County

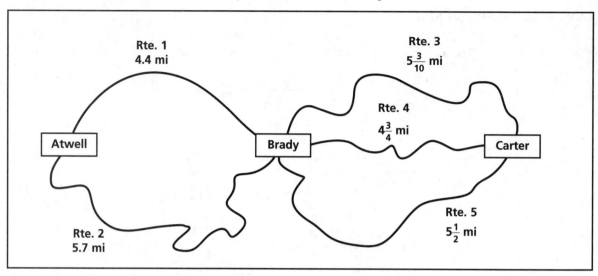

1. Name all the routes you could take from Atwell to Carter, and find the length of each route.

2. For a route chosen at random, from Atwell to Carter, what is the probability of traveling less than 10 miles?

3. What is the probability of taking a random route from Atwell to Carter that is the shortest?

4. What is the probability of taking a random route from Atwell to Carter that is 11 miles or longer?

5. Min left Atwell at 9:05. She took 6 minutes to drive to Brady. She arrived in Carter at 9:23. How long did it take Min to drive from Brady to Carter?

6. Tae left Atwell at 11:57. He reached Brady at 12:04 and drove to Carter. The whole trip took 14 minutes. How long did the trip from Brady to Carter take?

LANGUAGE OF MATHEMATICS

Complete the sentence. Write *likely, possible, certain,* or *impossible*.

7. An event is _____ if all the outcomes are positive.

8. In a _____ event, the probability is greater than $\frac{1}{2}$.

9. There can't be more positive outcomes than _____ outcomes.

10. An event is _____ if there are no positive outcomes.

The Range and the Mode of a Set

REACHING MY GOAL
Find the range and the mode of a set of numbers. (MA.E.1.2.2)

How did I do?

A. A set of numbers can be described in several ways. The **range** of a set tells how spread out the numbers are. The **mode** of a set tells which number or numbers appear most often. A set with no numbers repeated has no mode.

Example 1

Find the range and the mode of the set of numbers.

64   71   82   57   45   70   68   80

a. Find the difference of the greatest number and the least number.

82 − [   ] = [   ]

The range is [   ].

> **THINK**
> On a number line, the distance between the greatest number and the least number of a set shows the range.

b. Find the number that appears most often.
There are no repeated numbers.

The set has no mode.

B. Stem-and-leaf plots can help you find the range and the mode of a set.

Example 2

Find the range and the mode of the data.

9	3 8 5 8
8	1
7	3 6
6	0 8 4 0
5	
4	3
3	
2	
1	
0	

a. Find the difference of the greatest value and the least value.

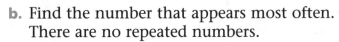

[   ] − 43 = [   ]

The range is [   ].

b. Find the number that appears most often.
Both 98 and [   ] appear twice, so there are two modes.

The modes are [   ] and [   ].

Practice

1. Place the data in the stem-and-leaf plot. (Note: the stems have already been written.) Then find the range and the mode of the set.

    Data: 113   86   97   121   113   100   91   82   99   115   113   97

    12 |
    11 |
    10 |
     9 |
     8 |

    greatest value − least value = range

    ▢   −   ▢   =   ▢

    The number that appears most often is ▢.

    So, the range is ▢ and the mode is ▢.

For problems 2–5, find the range and the mode of the set.

2. $\frac{1}{2}$ $\frac{3}{4}$ $\frac{3}{8}$ $\frac{9}{16}$ $\frac{7}{8}$ $\frac{1}{2}$ $\frac{1}{4}$ $\frac{3}{16}$

    range: ▢   mode: ▢

3. 5.7   8.4   10.7   3.8   11.9   6.7   5.8   10.5

    range: ▢   mode: ▢

4. 29   16   18   10   21   16   8   13

    range: ▢   mode: ▢

5. $6\frac{1}{8}$ $4\frac{3}{8}$ $2\frac{7}{8}$ $6\frac{1}{8}$ $7\frac{5}{8}$ $4\frac{3}{8}$ $8\frac{1}{4}$ $9\frac{1}{2}$

    range: ▢   mode: ▢

6. Write the set of data in the stem-and-leaf plot. Then find the range and the mode of the set.

    Data: 76   89   81   102   77   94   105   90   82   63   81   98

    ▢ |
    ▢ |
    ▢ |
    ▢ |
    ▢ |

    range: ▢   mode: ▢

Problem Solving

Use the range and the mode to complete the stem-and-leaf plot.

1.

	3
	2 3

range: 23
mode: 72

2.

	9
	6
	9

range: 26
mode: 49

3.

	7
	1

range: 21
mode: 14

4.

	4
	4
	8

range: 18
mode: 54

Solve.

5. Selena's corn plants had the following heights: 0.95 m, 1.1 m, 1.2 m, 0.8 m, 0.9 m, 1.35 m, and 1.05 m. What is the range in height of the corn plants? The mode?

6. Students in ten schools in Minnesota recorded the temperature at 9:00 A.M. on January 14. Find the range and the mode of the temperatures.

   Temperatures recorded: 7°F, ⁻1°F, 12°F, ⁻8°F, ⁻9°F, 0°F, 7°F, ⁻6°F, 3°F, 6°F

7. A chemist measured the mass of eight soil samples. What was the range and the mode of the masses?

   Soil sample masses: 0.5 g, 0.97 g, 0.83 g, 0.78 g, 0.55 g, 0.61 g, 0.49 g, 0.88 g

8. Lynne recorded the ages of everyone who attended her family's annual reunion. Find the range and the mode of ages she recorded.

   Ages recorded (years): 60, 51, 17, 7, 10, 37, 44, 7, 74, 73, 36, 20, 19, 65, 9, 32, 36, 54

> Could the range of a set of numbers be 0? Could the mode of a set of numbers be 0? Explain. Give examples if you can.

Connections

The Powells' dog had seven puppies. **Use the table to answer the questions.**

Puppy	Weight at 1 Week	Weight at 4 Weeks
1	$1\frac{1}{4}$ lb	$4\frac{3}{4}$ lb
2	$1\frac{1}{8}$ lb	5 lb
3	$\frac{7}{8}$ lb	$4\frac{1}{4}$ lb
4	1 lb	$3\frac{1}{2}$ lb
5	$1\frac{1}{2}$ lb	$5\frac{1}{8}$ lb
6	$1\frac{1}{8}$ lb	$4\frac{3}{8}$ lb
7	$1\frac{5}{8}$ lb	5 lb

1. Which puppy weighed the most at one week?

2. Which puppy weighed the most at four weeks?

3. Which puppy gained the most weight from week 1 to week 4?

4. Which puppy gained the least weight from week 1 to week 4?

5. What was the range of weights at one week?

6. What was the range of weights at four weeks?

Use the table and the clues to identify each puppy.

Clues

- Harry weighs less than Wanda. Harry and Wanda each gained the same amount of weight from week 1 to week 4.

- At week 1, Telex and Charlotte each weighed $\frac{1}{2}$ lb less than Wanda. At week 4, Charlotte weighed the same as Wanda.

- At week 4, Sam weighed $\frac{1}{4}$ lb less than the mode.

- At week 1, Stella weighed $\frac{3}{8}$ lb more than the mode.

7. Puppy _____ is Harry.

8. Puppy _____ is Wanda.

9. Puppy _____ is Telex.

10. Puppy _____ is Charlotte.

11. Puppy _____ is Sam.

12. Puppy _____ is Stella.

13. Puppy _____ is Fender.

• TOPIC 7: Probability and Statistics Lesson 9

The Mean and the Median of a Set

REACHING MY GOAL
Find the mean and the median of a set of numbers. (MA.E.1.2.2)

How did I do?

A. Another way to describe a set is to show where the middle of the data is. The **median** of a set is the middle number or—if there is an even number of data—the value halfway between the middle numbers.

Example 1

Find the median of the numbers in the box.

Write the numbers in order. 17, ░░░, ░░░, ░░░, 30

The middle number of the set is ░░░ .

So, the median is ░░░ .

	28	
24		
	17	
21		30

Example 2

Find the median of the numbers in the box.

Write the numbers in order. 12, 15, 18, 23, 37, 57

There are two middle numbers: 18 and 23.

Add the two middle numbers, and divide the sum by 2.

18 + 23 = ░░░   →   ░░░ ÷ 2 = ░░░ $\frac{1}{2}$

So, the median is ░░░ $\frac{1}{2}$.

57	12	23
15	37	18

B. The **mean** of a set is the number you get when you add all the numbers together and then divide the sum by the number of addends.

Example 3

Find the mean of the numbers in Example 1.

Add the numbers. 24 + 28 + 17 + 21 + 30 = ░░░

Divide the sum by the number of addends. ░░░ ÷ 5 = ░░░

So, the mean is ░░░ .

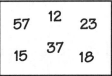

THINK

In everyday language, the mean is often called the **average**.

Example 4

Find the mean of the numbers in Example 2.

Add the numbers. 57 + 12 + 23 + 15 + 37 + 18 = ░░░

Divide the sum by the number of addends. ░░░ ÷ 6 = ░░░

So, the mean is ░░░ .

Practice

Find the median of the set of numbers.

1. 2, 11, 40, 25, 11, 28

    a. Write the numbers in order.   2, 11, ▢, ▢, ▢, ▢

    b. There are ▢ middle numbers. Add them, and divide the sum by 2.

    11 + ▢ = ▢   →   ▢ ÷ 2 = ▢

    The median is ▢.

2. 40, 50, 39, 36, 45

    ▢

3. 99, 63, 75, 100, 109, 77, 66, 71

    ▢

4. 58, 22, 65, 67, 33, 70

    ▢

5. 83, 64, 60, 64, 79, 91, 53

    ▢

6. 157, 235, 289, 160, 182, 216

    ▢

7. 1,203; 1,414; 987; 1,010; 1,655

    ▢

Find the mean of the set of numbers.

8. 9, 2, 7, 10, 14, 6

    a. Add the numbers.   9 + 2 + 7 + 10 + 14 + 6 = ▢

    b. Divide the sum by the number of data in the set.

    ▢ ÷ 6 = ▢

    The mean is ▢.

9. 55, 25, 41, 34, 70

    ▢

10. 20, 33, 46, 34, 17, 30

    ▢

11. 13, 12, 11, 10, 9, 8, 7

    ▢

12. 318, 340, 321, 329

    ▢

13. 40, 30, 90, 70, 50, 40, 30

    ▢

14. 461, 523, 490, 615, 576

    ▢

Find the median and mean of the set.

15. $3\frac{1}{2}$, 5, $7\frac{3}{4}$, $1\frac{1}{2}$, $8\frac{1}{4}$, 4

    median: ▢   mean: ▢

16. 17%, 15%, 3%, 25%, 10%

    median: ▢   mean: ▢

Problem Solving

Find the missing numbers.

1. Set: 25, 28, 12, ▢   Mean = ▢   Median = 24

   Think: To find the missing number of the set, I can work backward. I can multiply the median by 2, and then subtract ▢ from the product. Or, I can write an equation using a variable for the missing number.

   $25 + x = 24 \times 2$

   $25 + x = 48$

   $x = $ ▢

   Think: Now I can find the mean.

2. Set: 42, 6, 8, ▢ , ▢   Mean = 25   Median = 13

3. Set: 38, 19, 27, ▢   Mean = 24   Median = ▢

4. Set: ▢ , 15, 4, 23, ▢ , 7   Mean = 10   Median = 8

5. Set: 70, 50, ▢ , 65, 40   Mean = 60   Median = ▢

6. Set: 66, ▢ , 71, 80, 75, 66   Mean = ▢   Median = $72\frac{1}{2}$

Solve.

7. A girl wrote a number on each of 23 cards. She separated the cards into five sets, and put the sets on a shelf. A cat came in, and knocked one card from each set. **Use the clues to place each card back in its set.**

   Hint: Start with Set E.

   Cards the cat knocked down: ⬜35 ⬜90 ⬜30 ⬜82 ⬜46

   Clues
   - The mean of Set A is the same as the median of Set B.
   - Set C has a greater mean than Set D, but a lesser median.
   - The mean and median of Set E are equal.

Set A	Set B	Set C	Set D	Set E
25	81	▢	62	15
37	45	45		45
16		48	45	
▢	34	37	50	75
		30	42	60

What is so interesting about the set 2, 4, 4, 4, 6?

Connections

Circle the median of the set.

1. 5 gal   3 qt   8 pt

2. 49 in. $3\frac{1}{2}$ ft $1\frac{1}{2}$ yd

3. 125 min $2\frac{1}{4}$ h $\frac{1}{12}$ day

4. 1,500 mm   110 cm   1.25 m

5. $1\frac{1}{2}$ qt   2 pt   5 c

6. 1,600 oz   150 lb $\frac{1}{10}$ T

7. 0.008 kg   6 g   900 mg

8. 5 km   600 m   400,000 cm

Find the mode, the mean, the median, and the range shown in each stem-and-leaf plot. Then answer the questions.

Basketball Scores of the Eagles

5	7 7
4	6 0 4
3	4 3 6
2	0 3

mode =

mean =

median =

range =

Basketball Scores of the Lynxes

5	2 3
4	4 7 0 2 4
3	6 3
2	9

mode =

mean =

median =

range =

9. Which measure of the middle of the data—the mean or the median—is greater for the Eagles' scores?

10. Which measure of the middle of the data is greater for the Lynxes' scores?

11. Which team's scores had the lesser range?

12. Which team had the greater mean score?

13. Which team had the lesser median score?

14. Which team had the greater mode score?